JUAN RODULFO

Remain Silent

The only right we have. The legal aliens

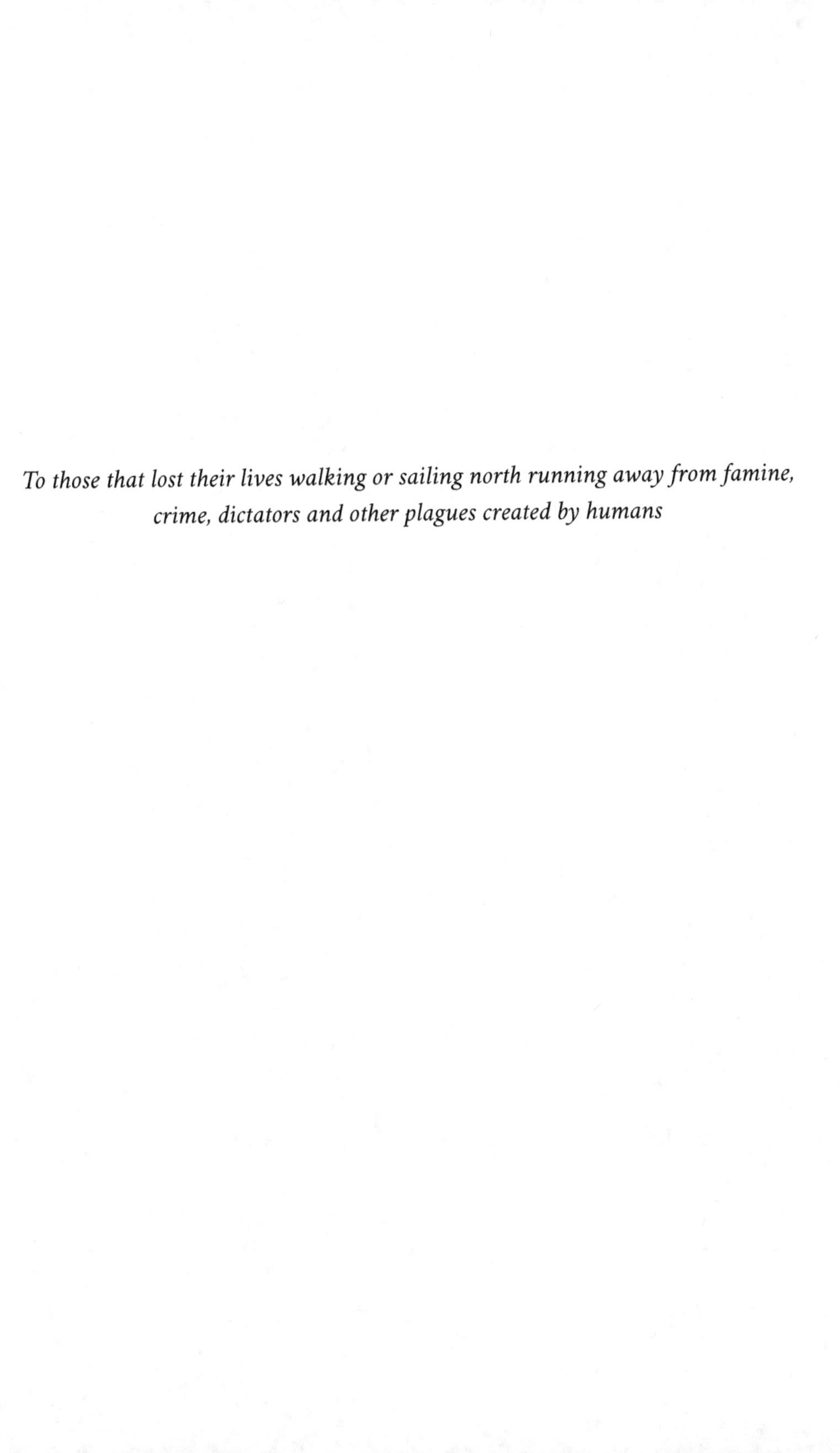

To those that lost their lives walking or sailing north running away from famine, crime, dictators and other plagues created by humans

Contents

Preface

One of the first books I published was "Asylum Seekers", based on the premise that "humans is the only specie on the planet that hunts, tortures and kills their equals for pleasure".

This was 2018, I was concerned about the migration crisis all over the world, and since that time until today October 24, 2023, I have been waiting for a decision on my Asylum petition to the US.

In that research, I covered the concepts of Asylum, its history, facts, how does it work in Europe, Africa, Oceania, Asia (gave special attention to the aggression against the Rohingyas) and America (By that time the Migrants Caravans were a thing), a assigned on full chapter to cover the Venezuelan phenomena, and ended browsing about the Universal Declaration of the Human Rights and the Bureaucracy, involved in an asylum petition.

By that moment "The Caravans" were groups of seven thousand souls, including men, women and kids, seeking their Human Rights to be protected.

According to Manuel Lopez Obrador, Mexico president, 10.000 migrants go to the US border a day, most of this humans are apprehended by ICE, stripped of all their belongings, sometimes violating their Human Rights, sent to Detention Centers and held in these centers, for days or months, to be released most of them with orders to appear in Immigration Courts, some of them are released with ankle monitors, some of them are released with a cellphone in both cases to be monitored 24/7.

After they are released, sometimes they are bused to the states, they claim to have relatives, sometimes they are picked by Republican Politicians and bused against their will to "blue states".

Once in US soil, released of custody, begins a ten or more years predicament with the hope in the government of someday, recover their citizen condition in equal proportion like the other immigrants that made it first into the United States of America.

Remain Silent means for me, the only right we immigrants have, since we had to abruptly leave the places where we were born to save our lives and the ones of our families leaving behind the few rights or privileges[1], remained in our birthplace to move here hoping to recover all or at least part of those sometime gained and enjoyed.

Well, all mountains look blue from far, told me once a friend, 9 years living in the US, I'm still only allowed to live secure, send my daughter to school, have access to an abusively expensive healthcare system, rent and own a house, work and other privileges granted for all in this country, I have no way to renew my Venezuelan passport, to travel abroad I need to pay and request permission to the Immigration Office, I have not seen my parents since 2014 and they cannot travel here, because they need a VISA or must be vetted by submitting a I134 form, which I already submitted for the daughter of a friend, back in November 2022, and today October 2023, I've not received an answer, my sister was assassinated and I could not attend her funeral, I'm grateful for all the guaranteed rights already mentioned, but what about the right to vote or to be recognized as citizen, which are primordial to move upward on the Maslow Pyramid of Needs.

In this research I try to shed light on the reasons why, us "the immigrants", in the US the "legal aliens", live in this "legal limbo".

On October 20, 2023, our daughter (12) was brutally attacked by another girl in middle school, she called us crying asking to be picked up at the campus. We rushed to the school, talked to the Dean and then with the School Police Officer, they expressed everything happened so fast, but they still promptly suspended the attacker. We had the choice to press charges against the other minor, but in a short exercise of reflection, we believed the suspension of the attacker would be enough for her to think over her actions and correct her path to adulthood.

---

[1] George Carlin, wisely used to called "rights" as privileges, since they are not 100 rights, as it sounds, they are just privileges given and taken on the government discretion.

My wife and I failed on our vote of good faith, later that day, we learned that the attacker, shot a video of the attack on our daughter, and posted it on Social Media, showing proud, no remorse and premeditation editing the video with remarks that she was happy of cowardly attack our daughter from behind, and then punch her unconscious in the ground, and send her to ER.

Does it have something to do with the title of this book? Probably, there is a component of hate in the criminal behavior of this teenager, is it associated with the fact of the color of our skin? Is it the same hate some politicians and business owners express at the moment of discuss immigration policies?

My father 88, since 2017 until today, has published 91 books, most of them denouncing the daily atrocities of the Nicolas Maduro narco-dictatorship in Venezuela, now I understand why is he so focused on his independent job, because, as Dave Chapelle cited the Care Bears shooting love from their chests when they find something so wrong, the same way my father facing so much evil in our country and in our planet, his best tool to project love and light is writing and writing and writing.

The same reason, I started this book the day after my daughter was attacked in the school and finished it 3 days later, to release mi anxiety, frustration, hope for justice to show up in our lives someday and to cooperate with my father on shedding light on the darkness.

Is there a light at the end of the tunnel for immigrants, refugees, displaced people to be treated equally, to be able to enjoy all of our Human Rights (privileges)? I have a dream that one day…

I

The Teddy Bear

Many countries continue to treat migration as a crime rather than a symptom, namely of limited economic opportunities and difficulty accessing safe, regular pathways for migrants.

Taken away

María and his 9 years old son Carlos[2], Venezuelan born[3], stripped of their Human Rights such as Freedom, Life, Security, Equal protection of the Law, Arbitrary Arrest, Arbitrary interference with their privacy, family, home and correspondence, To leave their own country, To own property, Freedom of thought and conscience, opinion and expression, To freely work, To rest and leisure, To a standard of living for the health and well-being of himself and of his family, including food, clothing, housing and medical care and necessary social services and To Education, by the Narco-Dictatorship of Nicolas Maduro and his partners in crime, the mother decides to in regards to save her life and the one of his son, travel to the US, in seek of recover part, or all of her Human Rights, sales the few she had, an old car, University Books, clothes, etc., asked her parents for money and gathers enough to start their journey from south to north, with his son, a back pack with essentials and her son carrying the Teddy Bear he received on his 3rd Birthday Party from his mother family, since his father abandoned him.

Riding Bus, walking, sleeping wherever they get caught by the darkness of the night, accompanied by hundreds of other Venezuelans, Colombians, Peruvians, Ecuadorians and even Brazilians on their pilgrimage to the US Border, they left Venezuela by December 23, 2022.

The Darien Rainforest was not something they could be stopped by, even

---

[2] These are not their names, but I met this family, and learned from them, their nightmare.

[3] I replaced the word "citizen" by "born", since there is not such thing as a human being called "citizen" and at the same time has no guarantee of his Human Rights…

though the dangerous it is for unexperienced travelers.

Carlos has been attached to his Teddy Bear for years, this unexpected traumatic trip, converted the doll into a more than needed emotional and psychological support for the kid, he speaks with the Teddy Bear like it's his all-life human friend.

Days and ugly experiences past by and they reach the border of the US, the First World, they're put in line with other hundreds, until it's their turn to face the border authorities, the first step once in ICE custody: Get Rid off all their belongings, the few she had into her back pack, some pictures of their families, their Passports, including the Teddy Bear, the passport are "confiscated" even after they are released, violating the few right they kept, like having right to an Identity.

The asthmatic attack, the crying screams of son and mother crossed the US border from west to east, but this did not stop the ICE to take away the kid's Teddy Bear and throw it to the garbage can…

Luckily, they were "jailed" together, spent the new year eve in "custody" of ICE, their crime: Cry for HELP.

Border Patrol

An August 1 complaint about Border Patrol agents confiscating Sikh asylum seekers' religious headgear is the latest example in a longstanding pattern. U.S. border law enforcement agencies often fail to return, or discard, valuable items that they take from migrants.

Upon entering Border Patrol or Customs and Border Protection (CBP) custody—whether apprehended in the field or voluntarily turning themselves in to seek asylum—migrants surrender what they're carrying. CBP's Transport, Escort, Detention and Search (TEDS) standards state that their belongings are to be "safeguarded" "documented" and held for 30 days or more. "After 30 days personal property will be considered abandoned and may be destroyed," the standards document reads, though it's not clear how migrants are expected to claim their property while in custody, moved elsewhere, or removed from the United States without it.

Far too often, property doesn't get returned. This is a longstanding unofficial practice of many CBP officers and Border Patrol agents: several years ago, a janitor at a CBP facility in Ajo, Arizona, even made an art exhibit out of confiscated items that had accumulated.

The pattern includes agents' confiscation of items vital to religious freedom, like rosary beads or the 64 or more turbans taken from Sikhs in Arizona so far this year. Some unreturned items have monetary value, like cash, jewelry, and mobile phones. Some have sentimental value, like photos, small heirlooms, and children's stuffed animals and dolls. Some are important for health and well-being, like prescriptions and medicines. And some are essential for navigating daily life as a U.S.-based asylum seeker, like identity documents, proof of persecution, and vital phone numbers.

Some unreturned documents can be essential to winning asylum cases and avoiding removal to migrants' home countries, where they could be killed. Attorney Chelsea Sachau of the Arizona-based Florence Immigrant and Refugee Rights Project discussed this earlier this month with the Arizona Republic:

"One of my first clients that I ever met with carried 500 pages of legal documents from his case in his home country. He wrapped them in plastic, and he left other things at home because he knew how important those papers would be to show why his country's legal systems had failed. And he did win his case. But if he had passed through Yuma today and had his documents confiscated, he might have never won."

In April 2022 WOLA launched Border Oversight, a regularly updated database of alleged abusive or improper conduct by U.S. border agents. It captures cases from media reports, official documents, and complaints from advocates based along the U.S.-Mexico border. We have now documented over 300 events since 2020, assembling a disturbing picture of "everyday," unaccountable abuse at the border.

Of those captured events, as of mid-August 2022, 13 involve confiscation of documents and 28 involve non-return of belongings. This is just the small sample of cases that we know about because committed individuals and groups at the border are recording them.

Here is a troubling sample of cases just from the past several months:

Confiscated turbans

An August 1 letter from the ACLU of Arizona, first covered by the Intercept and Arizona Luminaria, contended that Border Patrol agents in Yuma had confiscated at least 64 turbans from asylum seekers of the Sikh faith so far this year, including at least 50 in the prior 2 months.

These, the letter argues, are "serious religious-freedom violations" against members of the world's fifth-largest organized religion, most prevalent in India's Punjab region. "Forcibly removing or targeting a Sikh's turban or facial hair has symbolized denying that person the right to belong to the Sikh faith and is perceived by many as the most humiliating and hurtful physical and spiritual injury that can be inflicted upon a Sikh," the letter notes.

Citing interns at an Arizona migrant shelter, Arizona Luminaria reported on August 5 that "the number of turbans confiscated and discarded by Border Patrol is in the hundreds, far beyond the number reported earlier this week." In further reporting on August 17, the publication, citing the national Sikh Coalition and the American Civil Liberties Union of Arizona, found "at least 12 new cases of turban confiscation this month alone."

Torn up Mexican currency

On August 4, the Kino Border Initiative (KBI), which interviews returned migrants who arrive at its shelter in Nogales, Mexico, reported a significant case of non-return of migrants' valuable belongings:

Last weekend, ICE deported a group of 12 migrants to Nogales after being detained. Every person reported that upon their encounter with BP, agents took away all their belongings and said they would return them upon arriving in Tucson, which never happened. When they arrived in Nogales, their belongings still had not been returned. Items confiscated included money (one individual lost $200 USD), wallets, phones, and jewelry with sentimental value. One person from the group shared that he witnessed a Border Patrol agent take $3,000 pesos [about US$150] from another migrant and rip it up in his face saying, "This is trash, this is of no value to you here," before throwing the ripped bills in the trash can.

Family photos

KBI also reported on August 4 about a Mexican migrant whom Border Patrol removed from the United States without returning his ID and phone. Without his phone, he lost access to a large collection of irreplaceable family photos. Another Mexican man returned without his phone "did not have any family phone number memorized," and was left trying to contact relatives via Facebook.

Passports in the dirt

In Yuma, Arizona in May, The Guardian cited Fernando "Fernie" Quiroz, director of the AZ-CA Humanitarian Coalition migrant assistance group, who recently "came across a navy-blue Haitian passport and Cuban passports just lying in the dirt, and he said he can't begin to fathom why."

"Come back in 30 days"

In late April 2022, KBI reported the case of a Mexican woman who was expelled without the opportunity to ask for asylum.

She was detained by Border Patrol agents who confiscated her belongings, including her cell phone. When she was going to be expelled into Mexico, a Border Patrol agent asked her to sign a paper saying that she would return in 30 days to collect her belongings. She asked the BP agent, "How will I collect my belongings in 30 days? Do I have to climb over the wall again?" The Border Patrol agent just laughed and said he didn't know. Border Patrol also confiscated several other women 's phones from the same group. A few of them were crying because they did not know their family members' phone numbers to contact them. One young woman in the group was from an indigenous community in southern Mexico and did not speak Spanish. She had been separated from her husband and now had no way to contact him.

Only their shoes

An April 2022 report from Human Rights First, the Haitian Bridge Alliance, and Al Otro Lado recounted the experience of a Honduran asylum-seeking family whom CBP expelled, under the Title 42 pandemic authority, into San Luis Rio Colorado, Mexico. "The officers did not return the family's possessions, including money, luggage, and medications. They received only their shoes, which were soaking wet and covered in dirt causing painful blisters to develop as the family walked in search of a bus to take them to a shelter."

Seizing proof of rape

In March 2022, KBI reported about a woman whom Border Patrol expelled to Nogales though she had proof of being raped by her smugglers. The agent, she said, confiscated her medical document:

One Border Patrol agent insinuated that the woman was lying about the attack, and tried to convince her not to undergo a forensic examination that would verify the abuse. When she showed paperwork from the hospital examination to a Border Patrol agent as proof of the attack, asking that he not send her back to Mexico, the Border Patrol agent confiscated the paperwork and did not return it to her.

In the trash in south Texas

Rio Grande Valley, Texas activist and artist Scott Nicol frequently shares evidence of migrants' belongings trashed near the border wall, where asylum-seeking migrants frequently turn themselves in. He posted photographs in March 2022 of Cuban and Costa Rican vaccination cards discarded in a trash bag at a site near the border wall In Mission, Texas. On May 3, Nicol reported finding a Nicaraguan birth certificate, a cell phone, and a child's stuffed animal beside the border wall in Hidalgo, Texas. That day, the Border Chronicle featured Nicol's documentation of items he has recovered near the wall in south Texas. "What really got to me were the x-rays I found. They were for a six-year-old boy, and it showed a steel rod in his spine. It was obviously for an asylum claim. Why would anyone part with those?"

Scott Nicol
@Scott_NicolTX

Asylum-seekers' personal belongings trashed by Border Patrol beside the border wall in Hidalgo, TX yesterday.

There was a Nicaraguan birth certificate in the trash can, and a cell phone and child's stuffed animal nearby.

@USBPChiefRGV @SecMayorkas @POTUS

8:55 AM · May 3, 2022

18 Reposts   **5** Quotes   **25** Likes

Flip-flops in the cold

A January 2022 Human Rights First report discussed asylum seekers placed into the revived "Remain in Mexico" program, sent into Mexico without their belongings.

Multiple individuals reported to Human Rights First that CBP officers discarded their personal possessions and that they were returned to Ciudad Juárez in December 2021 under RMX without their clothing, shoes, coats, or medication among other personal items – in violation of CBP's detention standards. As a result, RMX returnees were forced to wear CBP-issued sweatsuits as they were returned to Ciudad Juárez, and on one occasion, Human Rights First researchers also observed RMX returnees wearing CBP-issued flip flops despite temperatures dipping to 40°F that day.

"This is no good"

An April 2022 report from Human Rights First discussed the 2021 separation of a 16-year-old Nicaraguan child from his parents near Eagle Pass, Texas: "CBP officers ripped up the boy's birth certificate, interrogated him about his age, threatened to imprison him for 10 years, and forced him to sign a document stating that he was 18." Noticias Telemundo reported the case in December 2021:

The mother, Luz Zelaya, says that she, meanwhile, had her son's birth certificate torn up. It is a printed document stating that the minor was born in a municipality in northern Nicaragua in 2005, issued by local authorities days before his departure at the end of August 2021.

"This is no good'. And ra, ra, he tore it to pieces and put it in the trash. 'You're lying to me. I'm not dumb,' he tells me," recalls Zelaya.

Unaccompanied children's passports

In an April 2022 complaint covering 2021, attorneys from the Immigrant Defenders Law Center (ImmDef) heard from migrant children who described CBP personnel confiscating their documents. A 13-year-old child from El Salvador had her birth certificate "confiscated and never returned to her." A Romanian 17-year-old also had his passport confiscated and never returned.

Prescription pain medication

A November 2021 report from the El Paso, Texas-based Border Network for Human Rights included the testimony of "A.V.R.N.," a legal U.S. resident who, though not taken into custody, had prescription medication taken away by CBP Field Operations personnel at the Santa Teresa Port of Entry in New Mexico, west of El Paso. After receiving leg surgery in Ciudad Juárez, a CBP officer refused to allow A.V.R.N. to take 10 Tramadol and Ketorolac pills, prescribed for pain, into the country. "The other two officers kept asking him to allow me to bring my medication since I had a prescription and it was only ten pills, which I really needed. But he refused, stating that the prescription was not valid in the U.S. and that the pills were like bringing in weed. That night I was in so much pain because I could only take Tylenol for my pain."

These are just a few recent examples. WOLA's Border Oversight database includes many more cases of non-return of documents and belongings, going back to 2020.

This practice is an apparent violation of CBP's existing policies. It reinforces a tendency among border law enforcement agencies to view the migrant population—which is increasingly made up of families, children, and other asylum seekers—as threats or potential criminals undeserving of dignified treatment. It raises serious questions about what happens to property, like cash or electronics, that is valuable and unlikely actually to end up destroyed.

CBP policy does require disposal of possessions that it considers unsafe, threatening, or unhygienic. This may describe some items, such as the clothing worn by people who have undergone long journeys in miserable conditions. But it beggars' belief that items like those described in the above examples fit that description.

CBP and its Border Patrol component are capable of storing migrants' belongings and returning them. WOLA staff saw it most recently in Del Rio, Texas in March: at a respite center for asylum seekers released from custody, all retained the backpacks and bags with which they had migrated, each with claim tags still attached to them. That, however, is the only place we have seen this: elsewhere along the border, we have only witnessed released migrants allowed to keep whatever fits in a small clear plastic bag bearing the Department of Homeland Security logo.

Most discussions of human rights abuse committed by U.S. border agents focus on severe events like use-of-force incidents, fatalities, vehicle pursuits, or family separations. Alongside these allegations, and happening much more frequently, are a host of "everyday," less spectacular forms of abuse of migrants. Examples include denial of food, water, or medical care; abusive language, at times toward children; racial profiling; misuse of intelligence capabilities; deportations and removals that place migrants in danger, and many others—including non-return of documents and belongings.

This kind of "everyday" abuse needs to stop. WOLA is encouraged that CBP Commissioner Chris Magnus responded to this month's ACLU complaint about Sikh migrants' turbans with the promise of an internal investigation, adding, "Our expectation is that CBP employees treat all migrants we encounter with respect." We uphold the importance of CBP and Immigration and Customs Enforcement (ICE) management responding thoughtfully and thoroughly to the list of questions about these agencies' handling of personal property that 22 members of Congress submitted in an August 3, 2022 letter.

We are further encouraged that activism around the "migrant belongings" issue is increasing. On August 4, the Border Chronicle's Melissa del Bosque reports, a group of Arizona-based organizations, organized by the Tempe-based Uncage and Reunite Families Coalition, held a press conference in Phoenix to launch an advocacy campaign. The groups demand that CBP and Border Patrol follow their own written policies and that agents be retrained—

and disciplined if they continue to confiscate or dispose of belongings.

WOLA will continue documenting events like these in its Border Oversight database, and alerting regularly about what we find. Credible investigations of complaints, and cooperation with Congress and other oversight bodies, are necessary to guarantee accountability for abuses and greater respect for migrants' rights. We look forward to a future when we might have far fewer alarming allegations to document.[4]

---

[4] ISACSON, Adam. Taken Away: U.S. Border Agents' Widespread Confiscation of Migrants' Valuable Personal Items. August 25, 2022. Visited 10/22/2023. Available at: https://www.wola.org/2022/08/taken-away-u-s-border-agents-widespread-confiscation-of-migrants-valuable-personal-items/

Federal Review

The federal government is reviewing internal practices regarding the return of migrants' property amid reports from migrants who said their passports, birth certificates and other personal documents were confiscated and not returned by Border Patrol, the Department of Homeland Security (DHS) told CBS News.

The department confirmed the review when asked to respond to accounts from migrants who told "60 Minutes" that U.S. Customs and Border Protection (CBP) officials along the U.S.-Mexico border kept their documents, despite agency policy instructing agents to return migrants' personal property unless they are fraudulent.

"CBP and [U.S. Immigration and Customs Enforcement] are reviewing their policies and practices to ensure that, once a migrant is released from their custody, their documents are returned to the migrant absent a security or law enforcement reason," DHS said in its statement.

In a story Sunday on the tens of thousands of migrants who have arrived in New York City over the past few months, "60 Minutes" reported that all but four of 16 recently interviewed Venezuelan migrants said Border Patrol did not return personal documents before releasing them. Attorneys, educators, case workers and volunteers in New York told "60 Minutes" that the problem is widespread, citing conversations with dozens of migrants.

The migrants' accounts also prompted Democratic Reps. Bennie Thompson, Joaquin Castro, Raúl Grijalva and Nanette Barragán to ask the Government Accountability Office, Congress' investigative arm, to "conduct a review" of CBP's "activities, policies, and procedures regarding the handling of personal property belonging to individuals in its custody."

"Media outlets and other organizations have reported concerns about Border Patrol agents confiscating asylum seekers' religious headwear as well as not returning or improperly discarding personal property belonging to apprehended individuals along the southwest border," the lawmakers said in their request on Friday.

In August, CBP Commissioner Chris Magnus announced an investigation into allegations raised by the American Civil Liberties Union those dozens of Sikh migrants had their turbans seized and not returned by Border Patrol agents along the Arizona border.

Border Patrol, an agency overseen by CBP, is responsible for apprehending, processing and vetting migrants who enter the U.S. illegally. It typically holds migrants and asylum-seekers in jail-like stations or tent facilities for a short period of time before deporting them, transferring them to another agency or releasing them.

A 2015 CBP policy that remains in effect calls for the personal property of detained migrants to be "safeguarded" if it is not determined to be contraband and instructs agents to "make every effort" to transfer said property with detainees when they are transferred, deported or released.

The policy also says that migrants' documents "must be returned to the detainee upon release, removal of repatriation or maintained in the detainees' personal property," unless they are deemed to be fraudulent. But most of the migrants interviewed by "60 Minutes" said Border Patrol did not follow these policies.

Beberlyn, 33, a migrant from Venezuela who crossed the U.S.-Mexico border earlier this year, said Border Patrol agents kept several of her family's personal documents, including their passports, Venezuelan identification cards, her children's birth certificates and her husband's driver's license.

"They took them from me. Immigration took them from me," said Beberlyn, who is now living in a New York City shelter with her husband, 15-year-old nephew, 12-year-old son and 4-year-old daughter.

Like other migrants, Beberlyn said border agents told her they would receive their documents during their immigration court hearing. But her family has yet to receive a court appointment, and attorneys said it's unlikely that documents confiscated along the southern border will be transferred to courts across the U.S.

"I do need them," Beberlyn said regarding the documents. Her surname is being withheld due to her pending immigration case. "Passports are very important here. To open an account, to identify yourself, and I don't have that document. I don't have the children's birth records because they took them from me. That makes me feel terrible."

Theresa Cardinal Brown, a former DHS immigration official during the administrations of Presidents George W. Bush and Barack Obama, said Border Patrol's reported failure to adhere to its documents return policy could stem from the soaring number of migrants the agency has had to process over the past year.

Federal officials along the southern border stopped migrants over 2.3 million times in fiscal year 2022, a 12-month span that ended on Sept. 30, CBP statistics show. The figure, a record high, includes over 1 million expulsions of migrants processed under a public health order that bars them from requesting asylum.

"I think that's in large part because of just the number of people, and the volume, and how quickly CBP is trying to basically get them out of their custody," said Cardinal Brown, the director for immigration and cross-border policy at the Bipartisan Policy Center. "They're not probably taking the care that they should."

Cardinal Brown said the trend is "problematic" for everyone: "It's problematic the government's not abiding by its own policies. It's problematic for the migrants because if they are losing documents that could help them prove that asylum case, that's going to make it harder for them to do that in court."

Maria, another Venezuelan migrant living in a New York City shelter with her family, said Border Patrol agents failed to return her children's birth certificates and vaccine records, as well as her and her husband's passports and identification cards. She asked for her surname to be omitted, citing her pending case.

During a recent check-in appointment at the ICE office in Manhattan,

Maria said she was told their documents were still in Texas when she asked about their whereabouts. She said her 1-year-old daughter's vaccination has been delayed since they longer have records showing what shots she has received and when.

Maria said she was also told her family's documents would be returned in immigration court, but she does not think she'll see them again.

"I haven't heard anyone say that they got their documents back," she added.[5]

---

[5] MONTOYA-GALVEZ, Camilo, COURT Andy, HOLSTEIN Julie and HANFLIG Annabelle. CBS News. Accounts of migrants' documents being confiscated by border officials prompt federal review. November 7, 2022. Visited 10/22/2023. Available at: https://www.cbsnews.com/news/immigration-migrants-documents-confiscated-border-officials/

II

The Scarlet Letter

The U.S. foreign-born population reached a record 44.8 million in 2018. Since 1965, when U.S. immigration laws replaced a national quota system, the number of immigrants living in the U.S. has more than quadrupled. Immigrants today account for 13.7% of the U.S. population, nearly triple the share (4.8%) in 1970.

Immigrant = Criminal?

The Scarlet Letter: A Romance is a work of historical fiction by American author Nathaniel Hawthorne, published in 1850. Set in the Puritan Massachusetts Bay Colony during the years 1642 to 1649, the novel tells the story of Hester Prynne, who conceives a daughter with a man to whom she is not married and then struggles to create a new life of repentance and dignity. As punishment, she must wear a scarlet letter 'A' (for "adultery"). Containing a number of religious and historic allusions, the book explores themes of legalism, sin and guilt.

The Scarlet Letter was one of the first mass-produced books in the United States. It was popular when first published and is considered a classic work of American literature. The novel has inspired numerous film, television, and stage adaptations. Critics have described The Scarlet Letter as a masterwork, and novelist D. H. Lawrence called it a "perfect work of the American imagination".

The immigration system in the US converted the fact of being poor, being human chased by dictatorships, drug cartels, organized crime organizations a Federal Felony subject to lose the Right to privacy and healthy life by being monitored 24/7, like the worst of criminals on earth, which by the way they are almost all freely all over.

Lauren Kilgour, in an article published at the MIT Technology Review, said that electronic ankle monitors were originally inspired by a Spider-Man comic and electronic monitoring equipment for cows, and initially developed in the US to enforce house arrest in the early 1980s. They're now regularly used in all 50 states and the District of Columbia to enforce supervision orders during probation, parole, and pretrial release.

In recent years, ankle monitor use has also spread outside the criminal justice system. They are now used to surveil immigrants who enter the US and Canada without documentation, to monitor truant teens, and to track elders affected by cognitive conditions.[6]

Humiliating

David Yaffe-Bellany, with the contribution of: Jay Root, Andres Torres and Juan Luis García Hernández, in his article "It's humiliating": Released immigrants describe life with ankle monitors, published on august 10, 2018 by the Texas Tribune, expressed that:

Every afternoon, dozens of immigrant families released by the U.S. government walk three blocks from the Greyhound bus station in this South Texas border city to a migrant shelter run by Catholic Charities.

Along with the clothes slung over their shoulders, the migrants sometimes carry government-issued containers — dark-blue receptacles resembling lunch boxes, with plastic handles that shine in the mid-afternoon sun.

On the front of each container, the black-and-white logo of the GEO Group, the for-profit prison corporation that operates immigrant detention centers in the United States, hints at the contents: power cords required to charge the electronic tracking bracelets that tens of thousands of migrant adults, including most of the asylum-seekers who come through McAllen, are required to wear around their ankles so that U.S. Immigration and Customs Enforcement can monitor their whereabouts between court dates.

Migrants are quick to acknowledge that they would rather wear ankle monitors than sit in a detention facility, and those who wear them almost always show up for required hearings, according to ICE data. But the devices can disrupt almost every aspect of daily life, from sleeping and exercising to

---

[6] KILGOUR, Lauren. MIT Technology Review. Covid-19 has led to a worrisome uptick in the use of electronic ankle monitors. October 8,2020. Visited 10/22/2023. Available at: https://www.technologyreview.com/2020/10/08/1009822/covid-19-surveillance-electroni c-ankle-monitors-opinion/

buying groceries and getting a job, according to more than a dozen attorneys, immigrant advocates and Central American asylum-seekers.

Jose Santos Garcia, a 27-year-old asylum-seeker from El Salvador who crossed the border with his 8-year-old daughter, Brenda, received a jet-black ankle monitor and a charger packaged in Styrofoam when he was released in McAllen at the end of June.

"At least for me, it's humiliating to carry it — really like some prisoners, on house arrest," Garcia said. "Just for entering another country, looking for opportunity, I have to carry this."

As recently as eight weeks ago, families who crossed the border illegally, often fleeing violence and poverty in Central America, were separated at Border Patrol facilities, with parents handed to the Department of Justice for prosecution and children transferred to shelters for immigrant minors under a "zero tolerance" policy enacted by the Trump administration in the spring. Amid widespread outcry, President Donald Trump ended the family separations in late June, effectively restoring a more lenient system in which migrant families are allowed to leave detention while their asylum claims are processed.

Conservative critics dismiss this practice as "catch and release," and Trump has called it a "disgusting" and "disgraceful" loophole in immigration law.

Adrienne Peña-Garza, the chair of the Hidalgo County Republican Party in South Texas, said she has concerns about the government's return to the practice. Migrants "are human beings and we need to treat them as such," she said. "But we have to encourage people to follow the law."

For these immigrants, however, release from detention does not represent a free pass into the United States. Even though they've been released with their children at their sides, asylum-seeking parents face a complex set of everyday challenges once they leave government custody — starting with the devices around their ankles.

"It's easy to think, 'Oh, it's just a little thing around your ankle,'" said Heidi Altman, director of policy at the National Immigrant Justice Center. "In fact, we hear from folks that it really feels like another way in which their liberty and their ability to live their life is being severely curtailed. And it's constantly present."

ICE spokesman Matthew Bourke described the ankle monitors as a tool to "manage individuals who may pose a flight risk, but for whom detention may not be the most appropriate option." He noted that ICE does not assign ankle monitors to children, pregnant women or people with certain medical conditions.

But for those who do receive them, the ankle monitors are a source of near-constant inconvenience. Some models emit loud warnings in Spanish when they need to be charged, startling immigrants in the middle of the night or embarrassing them in public places. One asylum-seeker who has worn an ankle monitor for more than a year — and whose lawyer asked that his name be withheld to protect his asylum claim — said he lost a job at a construction site after his boss heard the monitor go off during work hours and worried it could put other undocumented employees at risk of deportation.

The asylum-seeker said he has to charge the ankle monitor's removable battery pack three times a day to keep the device from blaring. The ankle monitor also prevents him from playing soccer or going swimming; although showering is permitted, the device can't be submerged in water.

"It does bother you a lot," he said. "It's not easy to be monitored all the time, 24 hours."

Between 2005 and 2015, law enforcement agencies across the country dramatically increased the use of ankle monitors to track pretrial defendants and convicted offenders, according to research by Pew Charitable Trusts. Earlier this year, disgraced Hollywood mogul Harvey Weinstein was forced to wear an ankle bracelet after he was arraigned on rape charges.

For its part, ICE began using ankle monitors in the mid-2000s as a cheaper alternative to immigrant detention, and now the devices are a staple of the agency's Intensive Supervision Appearance Program. Some of the migrants enrolled in ISAP are also required to check in periodically with ICE officials, and others are subject to unannounced home visits.

"These different steps can be combined together depending on the circumstances, and some can be quite intrusive," said Greg Chen, director of government relations for the American Immigration Lawyers Association.

More than 80,000 immigrants were enrolled in ISAP as of July 6, according to ICE. Nearly half wore ankle monitors, and the rest were required to report to ICE agents by phone. In 2014, BI Incorporated, a subsidiary of the GEO Group, agreed a five-year contract worth tens of million dollars to provide ankle monitors and supervise ISAP.

Immigrant advocates were critical of ISAP long before Trump became president. In 2016, a coalition of advocacy groups filed a civil rights complaint documenting a wide range of medical problems caused by ankle monitors, including bleeding, electric shocks and general discomfort.

One of the migrants featured in the complaint said the tracking device burned her ankle while it was charging, causing her skin to chafe. Another had to go to the hospital after her monitor produced an electric shock when she picked up a metal pan.

More than a year after the complaint was submitted, Homeland Security officials responded in a short letter that did not address the medical issues. At the time, Centro Legal de la Raza, the California-based group that spearheaded the complaint, did not have the resources to follow up with a lawsuit, said Aidin Castillo, an attorney for the organization.

Spokesmen for BI and the Homeland Security Department referred questions about criticism of the ankle monitors to ICE. Bourke said the agency considers "comfortability, flexibility and construction" during the fitting process. Immigrants can "follow up with their case officer after the initial fitting if they experience any subsequent discomfort or physical injuries," he added.

In at least some cases, immigration officers appear to be taking steps to make the ankle monitors more comfortable for migrants. Last Friday, as he waited in line for a Greyhound bus in McAllen, Hector Hernandez, 38, said that the official who strapped on his monitor earlier in the week asked whether he wanted it loosened.

"I feel that it's there," said Hernandez, who came to the United States from Guatemala. "But it doesn't really bother me."

Ninety-nine percent of immigrants enrolled in ISAP show up for their court dates, although the program is less effective at ensuring undocumented migrants comply with removal orders, according to ICE. Immigration attorneys and advocates acknowledge that compared with traditional detention, monitors are less burdensome for asylum-seekers and more cost-effective for the government.

"It is better for the individual just in terms of well-being," said Ashley Feasley, director of migration policy for the United States Conference of Catholic Bishops. "And it's better, in many instances, for taxpayers."

But that does not mean the government should strap an ankle monitor onto every migrant released from custody, attorneys and activists say. Instead, these advocates argue, ICE should enroll more immigrants, especially asylum-seekers, in something akin to the Family Case Management Program, an alternative to detention that the government launched three years ago to accommodate the wave of families fleeing gang violence in Central America.

Families placed in the case-management program, which the Trump administration abruptly halted in June 2017, were assigned social workers who helped them get lawyers, housing and transportation. Over two years, 99 percent of the enrolled families — who never numbered more than 1,600 — showed up for their court dates and ICE check-ins.

Bourke, the ICE spokesman, said the agency decided last year that ISAP, which costs roughly $5 a day per immigrant, represented "a much better use of limited resources" than the family case-management program, which cost $36 a day. Both alternatives are significantly cheaper than immigrant detention, which the Trump administration is seeking to expand as part of a broader crackdown on illegal border crossings, even though it can cost hundreds of dollars a day per immigrant.

"There's literally nothing at all preventing the immediate restoration and expansion" of the family case-management program, said Altman, policy director for the National Immigrant Justice Center. "It's just politics."

In McAllen and other border cities, released immigrants generally receive one of two types of ankle monitors, according to local advocates: a bulky model that must be recharged at an outlet, forcing immigrants to sit by a wall several times a day; or a smaller, sleeker version that comes with an extra battery that can be charged separately from the monitor itself. (Bourke said

BI produces multiple types of ankle monitors, but he declined to comment on the specific models, citing "law-enforcement sensitivities.")

When he was released from detention, Garcia, the immigrant from El Salvador, appeared to have received the bulkier model, which he tried to hide under the leg of his baggy jeans as he and his daughter waited at the McAllen bus station at the end of June.

"I have seen Americans go around El Salvador free," said Garcia, a logger and carpenter. "They don't have to wear bracelets when they come to my country."

Garcia said he decided to come to the United States this summer despite seeing news reports about the "zero tolerance" immigration policy. He said he traveled to the border in a van with more than a dozen others and requested asylum at a port of entry, arriving shortly after Trump put a halt to the family separations.

At the bus station, his 8-year-old daughter, Brenda, sat next to him, hugging a stuffed dinosaur as she rested her feet on top of the plastic box containing the charger for her father's ankle monitor.

"It's like a joke that I have to wear it and also charge it," Garcia said with a wry smile. "It's like a joke from the president."[7]

Stigmatizing

Electronic ankle monitors – increasingly used as an alternative to incarceration – are bulky and difficult to conceal, displaying their wearers' potential involvement with the justice system for all to see, according to a new article by a Cornell researcher.

Though these monitors have been widely used since the 1980s, their design has not significantly changed in 30 years, suggesting that the stigma of wearing them and the difficulty of hiding them could be intended as part

---

[7] YAFFE-BELLANY, David. Texas Tribune. "It's humiliating": Released immigrants describe life with ankle monitors. August 10, 2018. Visited: 10/22/2023. Available at: https://www.t exastribune.org/2018/08/10/humiliating-released-immigrants-describe-life-ankle-monitor s/

of the punishment, said Lauren Kilgour, doctoral student in the field of information science.

"With something like an Apple Watch or a Fitbit, or other types of broadly available commercial wearable technology, the goal has been to make it less conspicuous, smaller, sleeker," said Kilgour, author of "The Ethics of Aesthetics: Stigma, Information and the Politics of Electronic Ankle Monitor Design," which published May 15 in the journal The Information Society.

"But because that same type of visual work hasn't been done [with ankle monitors], it raises the important question: Why does this object continue to look like this?" she said. "Why are questions about aesthetics not more central in conversations about ankle monitor design?"

Ankle monitors are a multimillion-dollar industry that has emerged as criminal justice systems seek alternatives to incarceration. From 2005 to 2015, the use of ankle monitors for people on parole, probation or pretrial supervision increased 140% in the United States, according to a study by the Pew Charitable Trusts. Monitors use GPS and Wi-Fi to track wearers' locations, enforcing house arrest, for example, or to keep them within a certain radius.

> "There's a long, broad and profoundly prejudiced history of taking people and marking them in ways that are meant to effectively act as a type of punishment."
>
> Lauren Kilgour

Though the monitors are associated with criminal offenders, they've also been used for people involved with the immigration system – and have recently been proposed or ordered for people exposed to COVID-19 in states including Kentucky and West Virginia.

But whatever the monitors' actual purpose, their wearers are often presumed to be dangerous criminals, Kilgour said.

"Whether you are a high-risk or low-risk offender, whether you are involved with the justice system or immigration, and now even in the context of COVID-19, there is no differentiation in the aesthetics of the different types of models used," she said. "It creates conditions to invite prejudice."

Criminal records are generally available to the public but usually require steps such as searching for or requesting them from the appropriate agencies. By contrast, ankle monitors make this information freely available to anyone who notices them.

"Wearing an ankle monitor is a little bit like being required to wear a criminal record on your body," Kilgour said. "Its potential to compromise or complicate privacy may jeopardize opportunities to form strong social bonds within communities, or maybe to obtain or maintain employment, among other things."

Though some wearers might try to hide the monitors by wearing long pants, it's not always easy or possible, Kilgour said. The article included a 2015 quote from one wearer: "When I go to school, I worry my friends will spot it and leave me. I push it up into my jeans, hoping they won't see. But the higher up I push it, the more it starts to hurt: most days, my feet go numb. I try wearing bell-bottoms."

Kilgour links the monitors to a centuries-old tradition of shaming people, from the metal masks medieval women convicted of being "nags" or "scolds" were forced to wear to the yellow armbands employed by the Nazis.

"There's a long, broad and profoundly prejudiced history of taking people and marking them in ways that are meant to effectively act as a type of punishment," she said.

They also deputize members of the public into keeping an eye on the people wearing them, she said.

Kilgour said more attention must be paid to privacy issues caused by the data collected by ankle monitors, as well as to their physical forms.

"If you solve one problem, such as changing the monitor's appearance, the other one – invasive location and time data collection – is still on the table," she said. "Unless you holistically revisit the overarching ethos and dynamics of carceral surveillance, which are frequently power-laden and discriminatory, which animate these types of monitoring practices, you're not going to resolve the broader social politics that impact people's lives as a result of being required to wear this monitor."

Living in fear

According to Eileen Sullivan, from the NYT, one of the biggest reasons for the increase in migration is the number of failed and authoritarian states in the Western Hemisphere. Struggling economies worsened by the coronavirus pandemic, humanitarian crises and political upheaval have sent people fleeing their homes for a safer and more stable life in the United States.

For many migrants, including those from Cuba, Haiti, Nicaragua and Venezuela, the situation is so desperate that the risk of making the dangerous journey and potentially being turned away by U.S. officials is preferable to continuing to live in dire conditions.

"Failing states across the Western Hemisphere is the disease," said Jason Houser, a former top immigration official in the Biden administration. "The flow of migrants to the border, overwhelming our agencies, is the symptom."[8]

The fear of being illegally sent to jail for being opposed to Nicolas Maduro or Daniel Ortega or refused to pay bribery and being killed by the Colombian guerrilla, the fear to die of famine or lack of medical attention, has pushed millions of humans from south to north, not only in Latin America but all over the planet.

They reach the US, Italy, UK, France or Portugal, if they do not die trying, in seek of protection, of being recognized as humans, of an opportunity to prove they lives are worth and bum! The first they get is: Jail, and if released into the country (US) most of the times gets an Ankle Monitor, to be 24/7 monitored, to prolongate his fear forever…

The Guardian, published the article: 'Constantly afraid': immigrants on life under the US government's eye by Johana Bhuiyan:

Macarena had just put on a pair of skinny jeans when her phone rang.

On the other end of the line was an employee from BI Inc, the private contractor tracking Macarena's whereabouts on behalf of US immigration

---

[8]   SULLIVAN, Eileen. The New York Times. Migrant Crossing Surges Aren't New. Why Is the Border Overwhelmed?. May 10, 2023. Visited 10/22/2023. Available at: https://www.nytim es.com/2023/05/10/us/politics/title-42-border-history-immigration.html

authorities. The employee had received an alert that the ankle monitor Macarena was wearing had been tampered with, Macarena recalled them saying. They asked if she was trying to take it off.

Macarena was scared and confused. She was trying to make it out of the house with her children, she told the employee, explaining that the tight jeans must have moved the bulky device.

She'd have to come to the local BI office to prove it, the employee responded.

It was the spring of 2021 and Macarena, whose name has been changed to avoid compromising her immigration case, was two months into the Intensive Supervision Appearance Program (ISAP).

The US government program was launched in 2004 as a "humane" alternative to detention for immigrants waiting for their cases to be heard in court, a surveillance system that was supposed to keep track of people in the program while helping them access social services.

Selected by US Immigration and Customs Enforcement (Ice) officers, immigrants in the program are electronically surveilled through an ankle monitor, voice recognition or the company's proprietary tracking app until their court date and meet regularly with a case manager. Holding an exclusive, $2.2bn five-year contract to run ISAP for Ice is BI, a company that got its start in monitoring cattle and is owned by one of the country's largest private prison corporations, the Geo Group.

While ISAP has allowed some immigrants to go home rather than remain in immigration jail, the program is hampered by fundamental flaws, according to ISAP participants, their lawyers and sponsors, as well as 10 BI employees.

They say BI's technology is substandard, with ankle monitors causing bruising, overheating and at times sending out electroshocks and BI's proprietary app frequently malfunctioning. ISAP's structure is as flawed as the tools it relies on, they argue, with arbitrary requirements and opaque decision-making processes inhibiting the ultimate goal of the program: transitioning out of it.

BI referred the Guardian to Ice for all questions concerning its work on ISAP.

Nicole Peckumn, assistant director of Ice's office of public affairs, said on Monday that programs like ISAP "are an effective method of tracking non-citizens released from DHS custody who are awaiting their immigration proceedings".

The agency said ISAP was effective at increasing court appearance rates among immigrants facing removal proceedings. BI had received an exceptional rating for its management of ISAP at the time of its last contractor assessment, at the end of January, the agency added. Ice also said there was no proof the ankle monitor caused any physical harm.

The White House did not respond to repeated requests for comment.

'My skin turned red and started bleeding.'

Macarena followed her mother to the US from her native Honduras nearly 17 years ago, when she was just 16. She settled in Virginia, got married and had two kids. In 2020, police were called to her home during a family conflict. Revealed to be undocumented, she was arrested and sent to an immigration detention center, leaving behind her husband, eight-month-old son and seven-year-old daughter.

"Before I was sent to detention, I was paying taxes, we were working. I didn't want to lose my daughter, my husband, my baby boy … I lived in this country for almost 18 years," she said.

Four months after her arrest, Macarena was presented with a choice: remain detained until her court date or leave but wear an ankle monitor for a month. Desperate to reunite with her family, she chose the latter.

Soon one month turned into 10, with the impact of the monitor extending far beyond what she had imagined. The belt on the bulky black monitor sat tightly above her ankle and it was heavy, she said, making it difficult to walk. Sometimes the device would overheat, burning the skin underneath.

"I put a big Band-Aid or a sock between the belt and my skin because it was so hot," she recalled. "My skin turned red and started bleeding because it was tight and hot at the same time."

Ice said BI had conducted extensive testing of its products and had not reported any instances or evidence that the ankle monitors produced enough heat or power to overheat or shock someone. Ice did not respond to questions about whether the agency had independently verified the results of these tests.

BI employees repeatedly accused Macarena of trying to tamper with the monitor, she said, including the time she had been struggling to put on her jeans. Once she was accused of disconnecting the ankle monitor when she was lying on her couch, sick. "I'm here on my sofa with fever and coughing. I think I have Covid," she remembered telling the employee. "How am I gonna remove this?"

Over time, Macarena said, she grew increasingly distraught. She tried to get a job cleaning houses or babysitting, but she said people didn't trust her in their home when they saw her ankle monitor. She saw mothers pull their kids away from her in the park. She'd notice people pointing and staring at the device while she was out with her children, and she worried her daughter would hear people call her a criminal.

The burden of 'over-policing'

ISAP participants around the country told similar stories to their lawyers and their sponsors, people who sign affidavits of support to help with the immigration process.

Rosalia and Sarah, whose names were also changed to avoid compromising their cases, were detained when they sought asylum in the US in 2018, fleeing anti-trans persecution in Honduras and El Salvador. They were enrolled in ISAP after being detained and were fitted with ankle monitors. With that came other requirements: a BI worker would visit them every Friday – though they never were told what time – and their movements were restricted to the state their sponsor lived in. Once a week, they visited the BI office about 1.5 hours away.

Rosalia and Sarah's sponsor, whose name is being withheld to avoid jeopardizing the women's cases, described their experience in the program as dehumanizing and traumatizing. Once, Rosalia's monitor had gotten so hot she had to wrap it with a towel to keep it from burning her leg, the sponsor said. Another time, Sarah had missed a home visit because she had gone to the store before a BI worker was scheduled to arrive. He had arrived 30 minutes early and Sarah had been accused of working illegally, the sponsor said. Rosalia's case manager was cruel and always treated her with suspicion, the sponsor alleged.

"They were really trying to catch them breaking the law," the sponsor said. Nearly all asylum seekers show up for their court dates, they added, citing a study from the non-profit Vera Institute of Justice. "They really want to go through the legal process. So all of this over-policing and inviting the carceral system into people's homes is not necessary."

Ice said not all people in ISAP shared the same circumstances as the people evaluated in the Vera Institute study and that electronic monitoring technology contributed to the program's success.

Ice said BI workers were trained to be objective and not to assume that a person in the program is trying to abscond, work illegally or intentionally violate their supervision regimen.

Several former employees the Guardian spoke to said this had not been their experience and that while they had been taught that not everyone in the program had a criminal background, their training had included how to defend themselves against potential attacks.

Immigrants speaking to a group of non-profits including Casa de Paz and the Colorado Immigrant Rights Coalition in Boulder, where BI is headquartered, said they too felt their case workers appeared intent on proving they were trying to abscond.

"My ISAP officer treats me like I am a criminal," one immigrant told the non-profits, according to their report. "He yells at me. I feel constantly afraid that I may be doing something wrong."

Another missed a home visit and was told they'd be arrested if they didn't travel an hour and a half to the BI office to check in in person. "I had to pay someone $200 to take me," they told the non-profits. "I have no income. I am an asylum seeker and I do not have work authorization yet."

Frequently, the immigrants reported, it was issues with BI's own technology that made it impossible to meet requirements.

Instead of wearing an ankle monitor, some in ISAP are required to upload a location-tagged selfie to BI's proprietary app, SmartLink, once a week. The company matches that image against the picture the person took when they were first enrolled. But Google Play and App Store reviews of the app listed a wide variety of issues, including people missing their check-ins because their pictures wouldn't go through, the facial recognition technology had failed to recognize them, or the notifications hadn't worked. "Couldn't send a picture …" one review read. "Got a call and got told to delete and reinstall, I deleted the app and now I can't install it back. They blamed us for not sending pictures. Ridiculous!"

Alyssa Kane, the managing attorney at Aldea People's Justice Center, an immigrant rights organization in Pennsylvania, said one woman represented by her organization couldn't get SmartLink to work on her Cricket Wireless phone. When the woman had called BI to explain, employees had accused her of trying to abscond, Kane said. The woman had legal status and had been in the country for at least 15 years before she was sentenced to probation for pleading guilty to receipt of stolen goods, Kane added. But her technical difficulties were so bad that she was listed as not enrolled in the program and was given fugitive status.

"All of this is for a 55-year-old woman who technically still has legal, permanent residency and an application pending with the immigration court and has been in and out of the hospital on multiple occasions for serious health issues," Kane said.

Making matters worse are the program's contradictory requirements and its opaque decision-making processes, immigrants and advocates say. Requirements to transition from an ankle monitor to app check-ins, for example, vary office-to-office, but could include participants paying for a work permit if they're eligible and living in one place for at least 90 days. But participants report that ankle monitors – which are clearly visible and often loudly announce "batería baja" when they run out of battery – make it hard to hold a job and that few employers offer flexibility to go home for case manager check-ins. With no income, securing a place to live for 90 days or hiring an attorney is difficult. Participants have also reported needing to show BI a passport to make the transition, even though Ice had confiscated the document when they were detained.

It was unclear to participants and advocates how major decisions, such as immigrants' transition from one level of surveillance to another, were made. Immigrants typically wear an ankle monitor for a minimum of six months, when some are expected to receive work authorization. But many end up wearing it for an average of one to three years. BI case workers can recommend participants' "de-escalation", but it's up to Ice to approve the request. Two former BI case managers said Ice had only approved about 20% of those they recommended for de-escalation and had offered few explanations for its decisions.

Both Rosalia and Sarah were given ankle monitors, but only one had it removed after receiving a work permit. The other had to keep wearing it for several more weeks. They weren't given any reason for the discrepancy.

Former BI employees said it was these inconsistencies that drove people away before their court dates. "Some people never saw a light at the end of the tunnel and that's why they abscond," said Olivia Scott, a former BI case manager in Indiana. "There was no set protocol. So if you had a GPS unit on for three years, you've done everything, you have your work permit. What else is it that you need to do to get this unit off?"

Ice confirmed these decisions were made on a case-by-case basis and took into account criteria including immigration status, criminal history, compliance history, community or family ties, caregiver or provider concerns, and other humanitarian or medical conditions.

Having a lawyer appeared to help expedite the process to remove the device, some former employees and activists said.

However, Ice prohibits attorneys from attending meetings between their clients and BI case managers, according to the 2020 ISAP contract. Kane and Karen Hoffman, an attorney, said that made it difficult to ensure their clients had all the information they needed. Several of Hoffman's clients had been given wrong court dates, while one had erroneously been told they faced a final order of deportation, she said.

Surveillance fears

At least 182,607 people were enrolled in ISAP as of January, according to Ice data, making it the largest supervision program of any US law enforcement agency. More than 60,000 people have entered the program in the last year, according to Ice. The Biden administration is expanding the program to include new levels of supervision, such as strict curfews.

After wearing an ankle monitor for 10 months, Macarena had the device removed in the winter. Instead of being tracked through the monitor, she's now sent a text once a week, after which she has to upload a location-tagged selfie to the SmartLink app. If something happens to her phone, she has to show up to the office to explain.

Macarena's ecstatic about the change. But experts worry about the long-term privacy ramifications of her surveillance regime.

Macarena said she was told by BI employees the app is "always running" and that she always has to have the GPS on or else she could be put back on the ankle monitor. There's little transparency into what information BI is collecting through SmartLink and even fewer regulations limiting what data it can collect. Ice said the app only tracked locations during check-ins but did not respond to questions about why Macarena and others in the program were told it was always tracking them.

Privacy experts and immigration advocates worry the company could share or sell the information, and that the data could be used against immigrants in other law enforcement contexts even once they gain legal status.

"The way the immigration system operates is to make us believe that we have no other recourse," said Maru Mora Villalpando, an organizer with the immigrant rights group Latino Advocacy. "When people are out of detention, they think they're on the other side of it, but whatever company has a contract with Ice, we have to be afraid of."

Macarena is too relieved to have the monitor off to be worried.

"I'm going to do whatever they're asking me to do to not be in trouble and keep close to my family," Macarena said.[9]

---

[9] BHUIYAN, Johana. The Guardian. 'Constantly afraid': immigrants on life under the US government's eye. March 8, 2022. Visited 10/22/2023. Available at: https://www.theguardian.com/us-news/2022/mar/08/us-immigrants-isap-ice-bi-ankle-monitor

Miranda Rights

The wording used when a person is read the Miranda Warning, also known as being 'Mirandized,' is clear and direct:

"You have the right to remain silent. Anything you say can and will be used against you in a court of law. You have the right to an attorney. If you cannot afford an attorney, one will be provided for you. Do you understand the rights I have just read to you? With these rights in mind, do you wish to speak to me?."[10]

In the United States, the Miranda warning is a type of notification customarily given by police to criminal suspects in police custody (or in a custodial interrogation) advising them of their right to silence and, in effect, protection from self-incrimination; that is, their right to refuse to answer questions or provide information to law enforcement or other officials. Named for the U.S. Supreme Court's 1966 decision Miranda v. Arizona, these rights are often referred to as Miranda rights. The purpose of such notification is to preserve the admissibility of their statements made during custodial interrogation in later criminal proceedings. The idea came from law professor Yale Kamisar, who subsequently was dubbed "the father of Miranda."

The language used in Miranda warnings derives from the Supreme Court's opinion in its Miranda decision. But the specific language used in the

---

[10] MirandaWarning.Org. What Are Your Miranda Rights?. Visited 10/22/2023. Available at: http://www.mirandawarning.org/whatareyourmirandarights.html

warnings varies between jurisdictions, and the warning is deemed adequate as long as the defendant's rights are properly disclosed such that any waiver of those rights by the defendant is knowing, voluntary, and intelligent. For example, the warning may be phrased as follows:

You have the right to remain silent. Anything you say can be used against you in court. You have the right to talk to a lawyer for advice before we ask you any questions. You have the right to have a lawyer with you during questioning. If you cannot afford a lawyer, one will be appointed for you before any questioning if you wish. If you decide to answer questions now without a lawyer present, you have the right to stop answering at any time.

The Miranda warning is part of a preventive criminal procedure rule that law enforcement are required to administer to protect an individual who is in custody and subject to direct questioning or its functional equivalent from a violation of their Fifth Amendment right against compelled self-incrimination. In Miranda v. Arizona, the Supreme Court held that the admission of an elicited incriminating statement by a suspect not informed of these rights violates the Fifth Amendment and the Sixth Amendment right to counsel, through the incorporation of these rights into state law. Thus, if law enforcement officials decline to offer a Miranda warning to an individual in their custody, they may interrogate that person and act upon the knowledge gained, but may not ordinarily use that person's statements as evidence against them in a criminal trial.[11]

The American Immigration Counsel, on their website in an article published on September 28, 2016 by Ingrid Eagly and Steven Shafer found the following facts:

It has long been the case that immigrants have a right to counsel in immigration court, but that expense has generally been borne by the noncitizen. Because deportation is classified as a civil rather than a criminal sanction, immigrants facing removal are not afforded the constitutional protections under the Sixth Amendment that are provided to criminal

---

[11] WIKIPEDIA. Miranda Warning. Visited 10/22/2023. Available at: https://en.wikipedia.org/wiki/Miranda_warning

defendants. Whereas in the criminal justice system, all defendants facing even one day in jail are provided an attorney if they cannot afford one, immigrants facing deportation generally do not have that opportunity. Detained immigrants, particularly those held in remote locations, face the additional obstacle of accessing counsel from behind bars. Yet, in every immigration case, the government is represented by a trained attorney who can argue for deportation, regardless of whether the immigrant is represented.

The lack of appointed counsel may have a profound impact on immigrants' ability to receive a fair hearing. Past research has highlighted the importance of counsel for asylum seekers, and regional studies have highlighted the important role attorneys play for immigrants navigating immigration courts in New York and San Francisco. Yet, up to now, the debate about access to counsel has proceeded with little reliable national information on how many immigrants facing deportation obtain attorneys, the barriers to accessing representation, and how such representation impacts the outcomes of their cases.

This report presents the results of the first national study of access to counsel in U.S. immigration courts. Drawing on data from over 1.2 million deportation cases decided between 2007 and 2012, the report provides much-needed information about the scope and impact of attorney representation in U.S. immigration courts.

The main findings of this study include:

Access to counsel is scarce and unevenly distributed across the United States

Nationally, only 37 percent of all immigrants secured legal representation in their removal cases.

Immigrants in detention were the least likely to obtain representation. Only 14 percent of detained immigrants acquired legal counsel, compared with two-thirds of non-detained immigrants.

Representation rates varied widely by court jurisdiction.

New York City's representation rate for non-detained cases (87 percent) was a full 40 percent higher than that of Atlanta (47 percent).

Immigrants with court hearings in small cities were more than four times less likely to obtain counsel than those with hearings in large cities (11 percent in small cities versus 47 percent in large cities).

Immigrants of different nationalities had very different representation and detention rates.

Mexican immigrants had the highest detention rate (78 percent) and the lowest representation rate (21 percent) of nationalities examined. In contrast, Chinese immigrants had the lowest detention rate (4 percent) and highest representation rate (92 percent).

Immigrants with attorneys fare better at every stage of the court process

Represented immigrants in detention who had a custody hearing were four times more likely to be released from detention (44 percent with counsel versus 11 percent without).

Represented immigrants were much more likely to apply for relief from deportation.

Detained immigrants with counsel were nearly 11 times more likely to seek relief such as asylum than those without representation (32 percent with counsel versus 3 percent without).

Immigrants who were never detained were five times more likely to seek relief if they had an attorney (78 percent with counsel versus 15 percent without).

Represented immigrants were more likely to obtain the immigration relief they sought.

Among detained immigrants, those with representation were twice as likely as unrepresented immigrants to obtain immigration relief if they sought it (49 percent with counsel versus 23 percent without).

Represented immigrants who were never detained were nearly five times more likely than their unrepresented counterparts to obtain relief if they sought it (63 percent with counsel versus 13 percent without).

About the Data

This report analyzes the government's own court records in immigration cases. Using the Freedom of Information Act (FOIA), these court records were obtained from the Executive Office for Immigration Review (EOIR), the division of the Department of Justice that conducts immigration court proceedings. The complete EOIR administrative database included 6,165,128 individual immigration proceedings spanning fiscal years 1951 to 2013. This data was reduced to an analytical sample of 1,206,633 individual removal cases in which immigration judges reached a decision on the merits between fiscal years 2007 and 2012. The analysis set out in this report appears in expanded form, together with a detailed methodological appendix, in Ingrid Eagly and Steven Shafer, "A National Study of Access to Counsel in Immigration Court," University of Pennsylvania Law Review 164, no. 1 (December 2015): 1–91.[12]

---

[12] EAGLY Ingrid and SHAFER Steven. Access to counsel in Immigration Court. September 28, 2016. Visited on 10/22/2023. Available at: https://www.americanimmigrationcouncil.org/r esearch/access-counsel-immigration-court

Representation vs Orientation

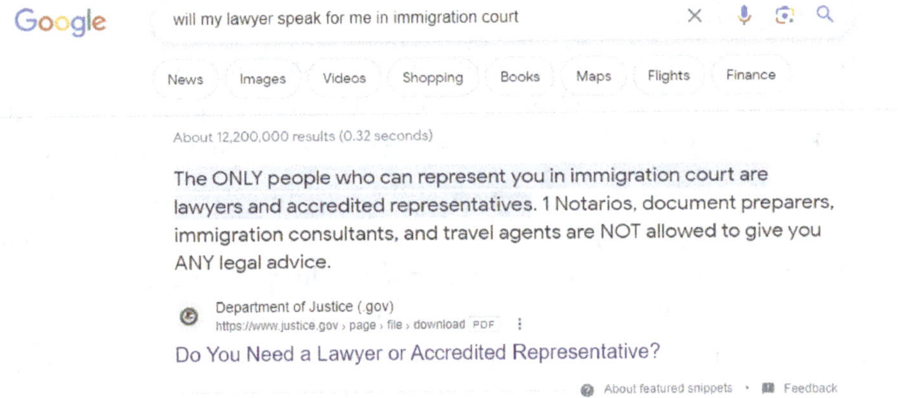

In a Self-Help guide published at the Department of Justice website, a Lawyer is defined as: "someone who has a license to practice law before the immigration courts and other courts of law in the United States. A lawyer helps you fill out immigration applications, such as an application for asylum. A lawyer may also help collect evidence, prepare you to testify in court, and present your case to the immigration judge for you."[13]

America Needs a Fair and Independent Immigration Court

In an AILA Document, numbered 21041931, dated October 20, 2023, is stated that: The U.S. immigration court system suffers from profound structural problems that have severely eroded its capacity to deliver just decisions in a timely manner and eliminated public confidence in its outcomes. The Trump Administration used these foundational flaws to manipulate the courts to their breaking points — pressuring judges to render decisions at a break-neck pace at the cost of accuracy, eliminating docketing tools, growing the backlog, and restricting access to relief.

On October 18, 2023, AILA's Past President Jeremy McKinney testified

---

[13] DOJ. Sel-Help Guide Do you need a Lawyer or accredited representative?. Visited 10/22/2023. Available at: https://www.justice.gov/eoir/page/file/1480736/download#:~:text=The%20ONLY%20people%20who%20can,give%20you%20ANY%20legal%20advice.

before the Senate Subcommittee on Immigration of the Judiciary Committee. The hearing was in immigration courts, an issue AILA has championed for reform for many years. This is Jeremy's second appearance before Congress. He first testified before the House in 2020 when AILA began its campaign to get the Real Courts Rule of Law Act introduced. At this hearing, Jeremy discussed his experience as an immigration practitioner, the pitfalls of the current court system, and proposed several solutions for improvement. Chief among his recommendations is the need for an independent immigration court and access to legal counsel for indigent noncitizens.

While we wait for Congress to act and establish an independent immigration court system, here are some favorable results of AILA's advocacy to help reform current EOIR practices. AILA garnered the following wins in the past few months:

- Cancellation of removal flyer: notifying noncitizens in removal proceedings that they may be eligible for cancellation of removal. This flyer also advises noncitizens of the visa backlog that will prevent them from getting their visa immediately after they win their case in court.
- EOIR Director's memo to immigration judges on DHS PD: This Director's memo was recently issued to guide immigration judges and BIA adjudicators to hold OPLA accountable for bringing PD options to a hearing. It specifically uses strong language to advise immigration judges that they should consider administrative closure over any DHS OPLA objections. It's a great source for practitioners to use in court when advocating for administrative closure of their cases (over the usage of termination), so that their clients can continue renewing their work permits.
- Notice of Proposed Rule Making on EOIR schedules: This is a proposed regulation that DOJ would like to codify. AILA is overall very supportive of this NPRM, and our comment will reflect this. It gives a lot of authority back to immigration judges and BIA adjudicators to manage their own schedules, dockets, and their cases. The brief history is that the Trump Administration tried to codify regulations that took away

judges' authority to administratively close and continue cases. It would have forced them to adjudicate cases faster (and risk due process) and gave the EOIR director authority to adjudicate cases. These regulations were enjoined so the previous, and better, regulations continued. This administration is seeking to codify these better regulations so that immigration courts do not continue to be at the mercy of administration changes.

- Language access in courts: EOIR issued a memo that addressed an increasingly common issue in courts – noncitizens who do not speak common foreign languages. There has been an increase in Indigenous asylum seekers and recent arrivals who speak rare languages. They are not able to communicate with judges in their primary language and a pattern of practice arose in which judges asked them to proceed in Spanish. This memo strongly states that immigration judges need to ensure that all noncitizens need to be able to proceed in their primary language and ensure that this language is available for all of their hearings. It also details that immigration judges have discretion to allow extensions and allowances for people to complete their applications for relief. It's a major step towards protecting due process in courts and we applaud this.

AILA urges Congress to create an independent immigration court.

AILA urges Congress to pass the Real Courts, Rule of Law Act (Real Courts bill) previously introduced in 2022 by Representatives Zoe Lofgren (D-CA), Jerrold Nadler (D-NY), and Hank Johnson (D-GA) as H.R. 6577. Unlike other courts, our nation's immigration courts are controlled by the Department of Justice — the very same law enforcement agency that is charged with prosecuting criminal immigration cases in federal courts. The Real Courts bill would create an immigration court system under Article I of the Constitution, reforming our immigration courts into an independent system that can ensure fair and efficient outcomes.[14]

The Real Courts, Rule of Law Act of 2022 (H.R. 6577)

One-Page Summary of Bill provided by Representative Zoe Lofgren's office: The Real Courts, Rule of Law Act of 2022

A hallmark of our system of democracy and the rule of law is an independent judiciary. Immigration judges issue life-defining decisions—decisions that may result in separation from one's family and permanent banishment from the United States. In cases involving asylum or other humanitarian protections, the decisions of immigration judges are quite literally, a matter of life or death. Despite this, our nation's immigration court system, housed under the Department of Justice, lacks procedural and structural safeguards that protect it against political influence and ensure impartiality and independent decision-making.

Immigration judges are not judicial officers—they are lawyers, appointed by the nation's top prosecutor, the Attorney General. As employees of the Department of Justice, immigration judges are charged with adjudicating cases in accordance with the policies and priorities of the governing administration. Each administration—Democratic and Republican—has used the immigration courts as a mechanism to shape immigration policy. Immigration judges have little say over the management of their individual courtrooms and the administration of their dockets, which undermines the fairness and efficiency of the courts as well as well as public perception of their neutrality and independence.

To solve these problems, the immigration courts require a structural overhaul. An Article I immigration

court system, like the U.S. Tax Court, the U.S. Court of Appeals for Veterans Claims, or the U.S.

---

[14] AILA. Featured Issue: America Needs a Fair and Independent Immigration Court. Visited 10/22/2023. Available at: https://www.aila.org/advo-media/issues/immigration-courts#congress

Bankruptcy Court system would ensure that immigration judges are free from political pressure and can deliver just decisions in accordance with the law. The Real Courts, Rule of Law Act of 2022 will:

- Establish an independent immigration court—known as the United States Immigration Court—consistent with Article I of the United States Constitution and comprised of a trial division, an appellate division, and an administrative division.
- Ensure that qualified, impartial individuals are appointed to serve as immigration judges at both the trial and appellate levels.
- Ensure that the United States Immigration Court has adequate resources and support to operate efficiently while giving the Court authority to appoint temporary immigration judges and establish temporary court facilities to ensure the expeditious administration of justice.
- Improve transparency and accountability in Immigration Court proceedings by requiring publication of all court rules and procedures, as well as precedent decisions and pleadings while protecting confidential information.
- Improve efficiencies by allowing the Immigration Court to establish its own budget without review by the Executive Branch and empowering immigration judges to control their own dockets and compel agency action that is unlawfully withheld or unreasonably delayed.
- Strengthen the integrity of immigration court proceedings by giving immigration judges authority to impose civil money penalties for contempt of court.
- Ensure due process by preserving the privilege of counsel, ensuring quality interpreter services, and mandating legal orientation programs for individuals appearing before the Court.

The Real Courts, Rule of Law Act of 2022 is endorsed by the American Bar Association, the American Immigration Lawyers Association, the Federal Bar Association, and the National Association of Immigration Judges.

AILA Doc. No. 21041931. (Posted 3/24/23)[15]

---

[15] AILA. The Real Courts, Rule of Law Act of 2022. Visited 10/22/2023. Available at: https://www.aila.org/File/Related/21041931b.pdf

How many of us?

I'm like 100% of world population am immigrant myself, particularly born in Venezuela and seeking asylum in US since 2014, with my case pending in Immigration Court.

Conor Finnegan, from ABC News, published the article titled: Where historic number of migrants is coming from and why: ANALYSIS, in his research, he found the following facts:

People are often fleeing economic and political crises.

In particular, data from U.S. Customs and Border Protection (CBP) shows that migration has recently skyrocketed from four countries: Cuba, Venezuela, Nicaragua and Haiti — all places where, as advocates and migrants themselves explain, people have faced crises of oppression, poverty, violence, lack of opportunity and a changing and dangerous climate.

"The Americas' ongoing migration event is not just a U.S.-Mexico border phenomenon. People are fleeing everywhere," Adam Isacson, director for defense oversight at the Washington Office on Latin America, a research and advocacy organization, wrote in a tweet this week.

Mexico and Central America still remain major sources of migration to the U.S., too, according to the CBP data. Mexico and Guatemala were the top two countries for migration, with Honduras fourth, in fiscal year 2022, which ended Sept. 30. The so-called Northern Triangle countries alone — El Salvador, Guatemala and Honduras — accounted for more than 541,000 migrant encounters, which was almost a quarter of the historic nearly 2.4 million total encounters at the southern border in fiscal year 2022.

CBP data on "encounters" is not the same as counting total migrants across the border — meaning the same migrant can have multiple run-ins with authorities and each is counted as an "encounter." Under Title 42 in particular, multiple run-ins have become far more common. Some migrant advocates say it's inflated the numbers and restoring regular order at the border, clearing the asylum backlog and improving immigration processing would reduce the numbers.

Either way, the exoduses from these four countries have hit historic levels.

There have never been so many Cubans reaching U.S. borders, for example. Between October 2021 through September, U.S. authorities have conducted nearly 225,000 apprehensions of Cubans, according to the CBP data. That's larger than the 1980 Mariel boatlift and the 1994 Cuban rafter crisis — combined.

What's different from those episodes, which sparked major headlines and U.S. policy changes, is that the majority of Cubans are now coming by land, not by sea. There were nearly 221,000 encounters at the U.S. southern border in the last fiscal year, according to the CBP data.

That's not to say Cubans aren't still risking dangerous water crossings, the data shows. Since Oct. 1, nearly 3,000 Cubans have been interdicted by U.S. Coast Guard crews, the military branch reported this week. More than 6,000 Cubans were interdicted in the 2022 fiscal year — seven times more than the previous fiscal year.

By land or by sea, all of them are fleeing an island further impoverished by the COVID-19 pandemic and struggling with shortages of food and medicine, political unrest, including crackdowns on protesters, and U.S. sanctions stretching back to former President Donald Trump. As the migration numbers reached historic heights in the last year, Biden started to lift the restrictions — critics say in large part to stop irregular migration — allowing for remittances once again, reopening the door to some travel and resuming migration pathways like visas and family reunification.

Neighboring Haiti has likewise been consumed by crises, forcing tens of thousands of its people to flee.

In fiscal year 2022, more than 56,000 Haitians reached the U.S., largely at the southern border, although many tried by boat and raft — often stranded and endangered — like 34 Haitians rescued on Monday by the Coast Guard.

In particular, there was a huge increase in September 2021 after Haiti's President Jovenel Moïse was assassinated that July and a 7.2 earthquake hit that August. But the number of Haitians leaving the country has steadily continued as the government, seen as illegitimate by many Haitians, struggles to combat rising gang influence.

In Nicaragua, authoritarian President Daniel Ortega's rule — and the resulting U.S. sanctions — have apparently contributed to the exodus of people as well. More than 50,000 Nicaraguans reached the U.S. in fiscal year 2021, but the following year saw a staggering 325% increase to nearly 165,000 Nicaraguan migrant encounters by U.S. authorities, per CBP.

October, the most recent month for which CBP has data publicly available, saw the largest single month of apprehensions yet.

No country has seen more flight than Venezuela, which has been riven by political, economic and humanitarian turmoil. The government of strongman Nicolás Maduro has overseen hyperinflation and economic mismanagement, has cracked down on protests and a political opposition that claims to be the legitimate government and, as a result, has been hit with crushing U.S. sanctions intended to try and force a resolution to the stalemate.

The U.N. estimates that more people have left the country than have escaped Syria amid its civil war and nearly as many as have left Ukraine since the Russian invasion — over 7 million in total now, or nearly a quarter of Venezuela's total population.

The U.S. has received a fraction of those refugees, but the numbers have been climbing to nearly 190,000 apprehensions of Venezuelans in fiscal year 2022.[16]

---

[16] FINNEGAN, Conor. ABC News. Where historic number of migrants is coming from and why: ANALYSIS. December 14, 2022. Visited 10/22/2023. Available at: https://abcnews.go.com/Politics/data-historic-number-migrants-reaching-us-borders-reasons/story?id=95198577

The African side

Nick Robinson, in his article: How the tide of migration is changing European politics, states the following: The number of boats carrying migrants from North Africa across the Mediterranean is growing fast - but Europe is struggling to come to terms with this mass movement of people. The BBC Today programme's Nick Robinson has spent the past week looking close-up at the impact of refugees from Africa all the way to Germany.

Tunisia in North Africa is now the launch pad for the majority of migrants who take the risk-laden journey across the Mediterranean Sea. There, I find hopes and dreams as well as desperation.

"I just want to be a basketballer," says Mohammed "BB" Lain Barrie, who has travelled 5,000km (3,100 miles) from his home country, Sierra Leone. "I know I'd be good," he says. "I want to make it for my family. My dream is to go to the United States to play basketball."

His face lights up as he talks. Yet just a few miles down the coast is a reminder of the risks he, along with tens of thousands more, is willing to take.

Fishing nets lie on the dockside of the port of La Lusa. But all too often the daily catch here includes the dead bodies of migrants who perished when their badly made boats sank or capsized.

Wahid Dahech is known here as the "corpse finder". People tell him when they find a body. He tells the authorities. It is his duty, he tells me. When some local boys went swimming recently, they came across the body of a dead baby.

Yet there is no shortage of people prepared to pay huge sums to get on those boats.

Most head for Italy. So far this year more than 72,000 people have made the journey. That's more than double the number who made it last year. The surge is made up largely of sub-Saharan Africans who are desperate to flee the continent.

And they are changing the politics of Europe.

Italy has a new right-wing prime minister, Giorgia Meloni, who was elected with a promise of a naval blockade - her version of Rishi Sunak's promise to "stop the boats" crossing the English Channel.

In Sicily, where the majority of those coming from Africa land, I speak to one of Meloni's allies - the newly elected mayor of Catania, Enrico Trantino. He tells me it's hypocritical to expect his home region to cope with the current influx of refugees: "It's impossible that they can come here and all of them can have the support they need to have a better life."

Meloni, once shunned for having roots in Italy's far-right, has now been embraced as part of "Team Europe". That's how she was introduced by the president of the European Commission, Ursula von der Leyen, when she accompanied her on a recent trip to Tunisia.

The EU is dangling the prospect of up to $2bn (£1.53bn) in support if Tunisia's president, Kais Saied, helps to stop the boats. That's controversial as Saied's been accused of stirring up racial hatred - earlier this year he suggested that there was a conspiracy in his country to replace local Arabs with black Africans.

It is not just in the Mediterranean that anti-migrant feeling is stirring. In Germany, the far-right AfD party is on the rise. A recent poll put them neck-and-neck with Chancellor Scholz's governing Social Democrats. And with important elections approaching, that matters.

Rosenheim in the German state of Bavaria - a few miles from the Austrian border - is the first stop for many migrants coming to the country. In 2015, thousands of Syrian refugees took their first step on German soil here. The country welcomed more than a million refugees in that crisis.

The local mayor, Andrea Marz of the conservative CSU party, tells me that with queues for health care, kindergarten places and housing voters can easily be persuaded that migrants are to blame.

The irony is that Europe - Italy and Germany in particular - needs more people. More workers. The government in Berlin is thinking the previously unthinkable and proposing that asylum seekers already in Germany - who are forbidden from working until their claims are processed - could be given a fast track into the workforce to help solve "desperate" labour shortages.

But just as business across Europe is crying out for more workers, voters across Europe are pressurizing their politicians to put their own people first.

The Dutch government collapsed last week because the governing coalition could not agree on new restrictions on immigration, and the once uber-liberal Scandinavian countries have also adopted tough policies. Denmark's Social Democrat-led government passed a law in 2021 allowing it to relocate asylum seekers to countries outside the EU while their cases are reviewed.

Few would not be moved by the dreams so many migrants speak of - whether it's to play professional basketball or to send money home to a struggling family or simply to escape war and violence.

But that sympathy for individuals has not turned into a collective willingness to open up Europe to those who want to come. If anything, precisely the reverse.[17]

From south to north

Western Mediterranean route

The Western Mediterranean route refers to irregular arrivals in Spain, both via the Mediterranean Sea to mainland Spain and by land to the Spanish enclaves of Ceuta and Melilla in Northern Africa.

Migrants transit through Morocco and Algeria to reach Spain. In 2018, the Western Mediterranean route became the most frequently used route into Europe. After the peak of arrivals in 2018, arrivals steadily decreased from 2019 onwards due to a variety of factors, and above all:

- increased efforts by Morocco to fight illegal migration.
- close cooperation between Morocco, Spain and the EU
- the COVID-19 pandemic

The European Border and Coast Guard Agency (Frontex) supports Spain

---

[17] ROBINSON, Nick. BBC News. How the tide of migration is changing European politics. July 15, 2023. Visited 10/22/2023. Available at: https://www.bbc.com/news/world-66202565

in controlling its external borders on the mainland through joint maritime operations such as Operation Indalo.

The officers, vessels and other surveillance assets deployed by the agency assist the national authorities with border surveillance and search and rescue.

In December 2022 the EU and African partners launched Team Europe Initiatives (TEI), which among other things focuses on the Western Mediterranean and Western African routes to ensure joint efforts by member states and the EU to address migration challenges. This includes a specific initiative that mobilizes €950 million to work with relevant African partners.[18]

Central Mediterranean route

Migrants and asylum seekers use the Central Mediterranean route to enter the EU on an irregular basis. They embark on long, dangerous journeys from North Africa and Türkiye, crossing the Mediterranean Sea to reach Italy, and to a much lesser extent also Malta.

The large majority of the migrant's transit through Libya on their journey towards Europe. This has contributed to the development of well-established and resilient smuggling and trafficking networks in Libya.

In February 2017 EU leaders agreed new measures to reduce irregular arrivals along this route. They committed to increasing cooperation with Libya and to tackling migrant smuggling.[19]

Climate Change Will Create More Environmental Migrants

The steady rise in global temperature due to climate change is making certain regions in Africa uninhabitable (due to water scarcity, intolerable heatwaves,

---

[18] EUROPEAN COUNCIL. Migration flows on the western routes. August 30, 2023. Visited 10/22/2023. Available at: https://www.consilium.europa.eu/en/policies/eu-migration-poli cy/western-routes/

[19] EUROPEAN COUNCIL. Migration flows on the Central Mediterranean route. August 30, 2023. Visited 10/22/2023. Available at: https://www.consilium.europa.eu/en/policies/eu-migration-policy/central-mediterranean-route/

and increased disease outbreaks, among other factors), causing a rise in migration.

Climate change is accelerating the pattern of rural to urban migration into Africa's metropolises. Between 2020 and 2030, Africa's seven largest coastal cities—Lagos, Luanda, Dar es Salaam, Alexandria, Abidjan, Cape Town, and Casablanca—are projected to grow by 40 percent. The dual strain of population growth and rising seas on infrastructure, agriculture, and access to water for African citizens in coastal cities will heighten the risk of governance and security crises.

Natural Disasters—from longer droughts to stronger storms and floods—are also contributing to a rise in migration. Over the last decade an average of 2.5 million Africans have been temporarily displaced each year due to natural disasters. The repeated damage to infrastructure and livelihoods impacts resilience, causing more to relocate longer term, even permanently.

Some African Migrants Continue to Face Acute Risks

An estimated 15 percent of African migrants, mostly those travelling without official documentation, face high levels of vulnerability to exploitation and trafficking, either along their route or in their destination country.

Libya, for example, remains a very dangerous country for migrants, with ongoing reports of murder, torture, rape, persecution, and enslavement of migrants by traffickers, militias, and even some state authorities.

North Africans still lead the number of Africans crossing the Mediterranean to Europe. The continued backsliding of democratic institutions and economic hardship in North African countries like Tunisia, Egypt, Algeria, and Libya will likely lead more people to look toward Europe.

Africa has documented more than 9,000 migration-related deaths since 2014. More than 25,000 have also disappeared crossing the waters between Africa and Europe.

Many countries continue to treat migration as a crime rather than a symptom, namely of limited economic opportunities and difficulty accessing safe, regular pathways for migrants.[20]

---

20 AFRICA CENTER FOR STRATEGIC STUDIES. African Migration Trends to Watch in 2023. January 9, 2023. Visited 10/22/2023. Available at: https://africacenter.org/spotlight/african -migration-trends-to-watch-in-2023/

A new population with no rights at all

Global forced displacement

At the end of 2022, 108.4 million people worldwide were forcibly displaced as a result of persecution, conflict, violence, human rights violations and events seriously disturbing public order.

This represents an increase of 19 million people compared to the end of 2021 – more than the populations of Ecuador, the Netherlands (Kingdom of the) or Somalia. It is also the largest ever increase between years according to UNHCR's statistics on forced displacement.

> More than 1 in every 74 people on Earth has been forced to flee.

Ongoing and new conflicts have driven forced displacement across the globe. The Russian Federation's full-scale invasion of Ukraine in February 2022 created the fastest displacement crisis, and one of the largest, since the Second World War. At the end of 2022, a total of 11.6 million Ukrainians remained displaced, including 5.9 million within their country and 5.7 million who fled to neighboring countries and beyond.

Conflict and insecurity in other parts of the world either continued or was reignited, such as in the Democratic Republic of the Congo, Ethiopia and Myanmar, where more than 1 million people were displaced within each country.

Refugees, asylum-seekers and others in need of international protection displaced during each year | 1975 – 2022

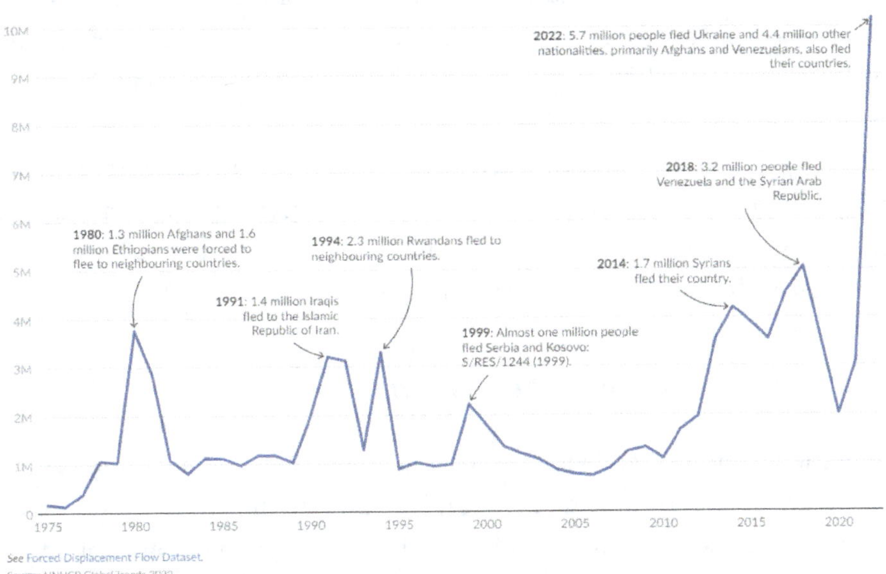

Number of refugees in the world

The number of refugees worldwide increased from 27.1 million in 2021 to 35.3 million at the end of 2022, the largest yearly increase ever recorded, according to UNHCR's statistics on forced displacement.

The increase was largely due to refugees from Ukraine fleeing the international armed conflict in their country.

Overall, 52 per cent of all refugees and other people in need of international protection came from just three countries: the Syrian Arab Republic (6.5 million), Ukraine (5.7 million) and Afghanistan (5.7 million).

Internally Displaced People (IDPs)

Most people who are forced to flee never cross an international border, remaining displaced within their own countries. Known as internally displaced people, or IDPs, they account for 58 per cent of all forcibly displaced people.

The largest number of people displaced within their own country was 6.8 million in Syria, consistent with the end of the previous year. This means that 1 in 3 of all Syrians remaining within their country were still internally displaced at the end of 2022, after more than a decade of conflict.

Displacement in the context of disasters

In addition to conflict and violence, people were displaced within their countries due to disasters. During the year, 32.6 million internal displacements due to disasters were reported, with 8.7 million people remaining displaced at the end of 2022, according to the Internal Displacement Monitoring Centre. Disaster related internal displacement accounted for more than half (54 per cent) of all new displacements in 2022.[21]

These people, around 140 million humans, lost the few rights they may have in their countries, like an identity and sometimes the right to vote. This empty space is promptly taken advantage of by dictatorial and narco-states. Now they are in a foreign country, with few rights guaranteed, and the right to be a citizen again, is most of the time something inconceivable, they (we) become into a new kind of human population with no citizenship (The Merriam-Webster dictionary defines citizen as: an inhabitant of a city or town especially: one entitled to the rights and privileges of a freeman), recipients of just a few rights.

---

[21] UNHCR. Global Trends. Visited 10/23/2023. Available at: https://www.unhcr.org/us/glob al-trends

I want to work, of course, but may I have my other rights back?

The US government, through the Biden administration pushed and made some adjustments in issues like allowing certain batches of immigrants to opt for a TPS (Temporary Protected Status) and made an increase in the years a working permit last for certain immigration categories, being the C8 (Asylum Applicants) in between others positively impacted, extending their permission to work from two to five years.

According to Transactional Records Access Clearinghouse (TRAC), an organization at Syracuse University, the approximately 650 immigration judges carry a backlog of more than 2.4 million cases in the US.[22]

Tae Johnson, ICE's acting director, states that there is a 10 year wait lapse in immigration cases in the US.[23]

According to the Department of Homeland Security (DHS), more than 350,000 TPS holders from 17 countries live in the U.S. today. With recent TPS designations and redesignations, however, the number of individuals eligible for TPS, those who have not formally applied or been approved, is significantly higher. In fact, FWD.us estimates that about 350,000 additional individuals are currently eligible for TPS; in all, nearly 900,000 individuals were TPS holders or were eligible for TPS protections at the end of 2022.[24]

As of December 31, 2022, there were roughly 580,000 active DACA recipients in the U.S. Over one in four (28%) active DACA recipients reside in California, with another 17% living in Texas, 5% in Illinois, 4% in New York,

---

[22] AFP. The Economist Times. For asylum seekers, giant US immigration backlog can be a boon. July 23, 2023. Visited 10/23/2023. Available at: https://economictimes.indiatimes.co m/nri/migrate/for-asylum-seekers-giant-us-immigration-backlog-can-be-a-boon/articlesh ow/102042534.cms?from=mdr

[23] SPAGAT, Elliot. AP. Immigrants waiting 10 years in US just to get a court date. April 26, 2023. Visited 10/23/2023. Available at: https://apnews.com/article/immigration-courts-wa it-54bb5f7c18c4c37c6ca7f28231ff0edf

[24] FWD.US. Temporary Protected Status (TPS) 5 Things to know. February 16, 2023. Visited 10/23/2023. Available at: https://www.fwd.us/news/temporary-protected-status-tps-5-thi ngs-to-know/

4% in Florida, and the remaining 42% distributed in other states across the country (Figure 1). DACA recipients are young with the majority under age 36 and over half are female. Seven in ten DACA recipients are single, while nearly three in ten are married. The top countries of birth for active DACA recipients include Mexico (81%), El Salvador (4%), and Guatemala (3%).[25]

This is 2.4 million asylum applicants plus 900.000 TPS holders and 580.000 DACA recipients, 3.880.000 humans[26], equivalent to the population of Los Angeles, CA., second mayor city in the US, in terms of population. We've been around since 1991[27], giving our share to the US economy, culture and history, I agree that we immigrants must be grateful with the rights (privileges) had been granted to us, like the right to have a job, and the right to have Healht Care, and send our kids to schools, and walk-speak-travel free to the inside of the country, but subjected to a travel authorization to travel abroad. Having all these rights guaranteed, I can tell you that most of US (immigrants) achieved the first stage of the Maslow Pyramid of Needs, but what about the other rights (privileges), like the right to be free and equal, freedom from discrimination, right to equality before the law, right to privacy, freedom of movement, right to nationality and the freedom to partake in public affairs?.

---

[25] KFF. Key Facts on Deferred Action for Childhood Arrivals (DACA). April 13, 2023. Visited 10/23/2023. Available at: https://www.kff.org/racial-equity-and-health-policy/fact-sheet/key-facts-on-deferred-action-for-childhood-arrivals-daca/

[26] Merriam-Webster Dictionary: Citizen: 2 : an inhabitant of a city or town, especially : **one entitled to the rights and privileges of a freeman**

[27] The first TPS was granted in September 16, 1991 to Somalia; in response to the ongoing Somali Civil War, and is scheduled to end on September 17, 2024

We pay taxes too

The United States was built, in part, by immigrants—and the nation has long been the beneficiary of the new energy and ingenuity that immigrants bring. Today, 14 percent of the nation's residents are foreign-born, over half of whom are naturalized U.S. citizens. Nearly 70 percent of all immigrants, who come from diverse backgrounds across the globe, report speaking English well or very well.

Immigrants make up significant shares of the U.S. workforce in a range of industries, accounting for over two-fifths of all farming, fishing, and forestry workers—as well as one quarter of those working in computer and math sciences. The highest number of immigrants work in the health care and social assistance industry, with over 4 million immigrants providing these services. As workers, business owners, taxpayers, and neighbors, immigrants are an integral part of the country's diverse and thriving communities and make extensive contributions that benefit all.

One in seven U.S. residents is an immigrant, while one in eight residents is a native-born U.S. citizen with at least one immigrant parent.

- In 2019, 44.9 million immigrants (foreign-born individuals) comprised 14 percent of the national population.
- The United States was home to 22.0 million women, 20.4 million men, and 2.5 million children who were immigrants.
- The top countries of origin for immigrants were Mexico (24 percent of immigrants), India (6 percent), China (5 percent), the Philippines (4.5 percent), and El Salvador (3 percent).
- In 2019, 38.3 million people in the United States (12 percent of the country's population) were native-born Americans who had at least one immigrant parent.

Over half of all immigrants in the United States are naturalized citizens.

- As of 2019, 23.2 million immigrants (52 percent) had naturalized, and 8.1 million immigrants were eligible to become naturalized U.S. citizens.
- The majority of immigrants (69 percent) reported speaking English "well" or "very well."

Immigrants in the United States contribute billions of dollars in taxes.

Immigrant-led households across the United States contributed a total of $330.7 billion in federal taxes and $161.7 billion in combined state and local taxes in 2019.

Households headed by undocumented immigrants in the United States paid an estimated $18.9 billion in federal taxes and $11.7 billion in combined state and local taxes in 2019.

Households headed by DACA recipients and those meeting the eligibility requirements for DACA paid an estimated $3.4 billion in federal taxes and $2.7 billion in combined state and local taxes in 2019.

As consumers, immigrants add over a trillion dollars to the U.S. economy.

In the United States, residents of immigrant-led households had $1.3 trillion in collective spending power (after-tax income) in 2019.

Immigrant entrepreneurs in the United States generate tens of billions of dollars in business revenue.

3.2 million immigrant business owners accounted for 22 percent of all self-employed U.S. residents in 2019 and generated $86.3 billion in business income.[28]

Undocumented immigrants comprised 5 percent of the workforce in 2017.

Steven Hubbard, in his article "Dispelling the Myth: How Undocumented Immigrants Pay Taxes and Contribute to the US Tax Base", found that: as Tax Day approaches, it is important to acknowledge the tax contributions made by immigrants—even those who are undocumented. These contributions play a vital role in the funding and sustainability of America's public services and programs.

Immigrants' Tax Contributions

Undocumented immigrants make significant contributions to the U.S. tax system by paying sales, income, and property taxes.

In 2021 alone, these households contributed $30.8 billion in total taxes,

---

28 AMERICAN IMMIGRATION COUNCIL. Fact Sheet Immigrants in the United States. September 21, 2021. Visited 10/23/2023. Available at: https://www.americanimmigrationc ouncil.org/research/immigrants-in-the-united-states

including $18.6 billion in federal income taxes and $12.2 billion in state and local taxes, based on data from the American Community Survey.

Individual Tax Identification Numbers

At least 50% of undocumented immigrant households file income tax returns using Individual Tax Identification Numbers (ITINs), according to the Institute on Taxation and Economic Policy. ITINs are tax processing numbers issued by the Internal Revenue Service, allowing more people to contribute to the tax system and build the tax base.

While undocumented immigrants file taxes using an ITIN, other people may also obtain one, including legal permanent residents, foreign nationals working in the United States, and immigrant spouses of U.S. citizens, among others.

In 2015, 4.4 million ITIN filers paid over $5.5 billion in payroll and Medicare taxes and $23.6 billion in total taxes, according to the IRS.

Tax Benefits

ITIN holders are not eligible for all the tax benefits and public benefits that U.S. citizens and other taxpayers can receive. For example, they are not eligible for Social Security benefits or the Earned Income Tax Credit (EITC). It's critical to remember that ITIN holders pay taxes to these and other programs, like Medicare and Medicaid, that Americans use every day.

If an ITIN holder becomes eligible for Social Security in the future (such as by becoming a lawful permanent resident), the earnings reported with an ITIN may count toward their eligibility. However, if they never become eligible, they cannot collect on their contributions.

Many undocumented immigrants have taxes deducted from their paychecks, even if they do not file income tax returns.

It is important to recognize that undocumented immigrants are paying their fair share toward the public good and hope that one day, they too will benefit from their contributions, just like millions of other Americans who file their taxes and fulfill their civic duty.[29]

---

29 HUBBARD, Steven. IMMIGRATION IMPACT, Dispelling the Myth: How Undocumented Immigrants Pay Taxes and Contribute to the US Tax Base. March 22, 2023. Available at: https://immigrationimpact.com/2023/03/22/how-undocumented-immigrants-pay-taxes-it in/

III

Glass ceiling

A glass ceiling is a metaphor usually applied to people of marginalized genders, used to represent an invisible barrier that prevents an oppressed demographic from rising beyond a certain level in a hierarchy. No matter how invisible the glass ceiling is expressed, it is actually an obstacle difficult to overcome. The metaphor was coined by Marilyn Loden during a speech in 1978. Is there a glass ceiling for immigrants too?

Cheap workforce

The cheap and silent work force

Salma Sosa of the Roosevelt House, Public Policy Institute at Hunter College, expresses that: The Trump Administration is not the first administration that has shown their true feelings toward immigrant communities. Regardless of party allegiance, every president has enacted xenophobic policies – even the ones we consider as "progressive."

One of these xenophobic policies was the Mexican Repatriation. From the late 1920s to the early 1930s, the U.S. government deported more than one million individuals who had any Mexican ancestry regardless of their immigration status. This policy, enacted during a time of economic struggle, used Mexican Americans as scapegoats who could be blamed for the devastating economic crash. In 1954, there was Operation Wetback, which was one of the largest mass deportations of undocumented workers at the time. Under the Eisenhower-era immigration policy, 1.3 million deportations were processed, and xenophobia was out in the open, starting with the name of the operation.

Americans tend to forget the type of immigration policies adopted by the United States demonstrate its xenophilic nature. We love immigrants when it comes to exploiting their cheap labor. The xenophobia aspect comes when they see the same exploited immigrants fighting back. An example of this is the Bracero Program —where the United States, in collaboration with the Mexican government, established a guest-worker program in 1942.

The program allowed Mexican citizens to work in the United States for agricultural companies to meet the food supply needs during World War II. These jobs were low-paying agricultural jobs, but these Braceros were "promised" a sense of stability with housing, transportation, decent pay, insurance, and meals. However, these workers faced countless abuses. Companies participating in the program treated them horribly and did not fulfill the promises they made to their immigrant labor force. For example, agricultural companies withheld 10% of their paychecks to be placed into a savings account, which could be accessed upon returning to Mexico. However, most of the Braceros did not receive the missing 10% of their paycheck when they went back home. Furthermore, Braceros workers faced xenophobic rhetoric from American workers and their bosses.

The Braceros program ended in 1964, under President John F. Kennedy due to the belief that it was negatively affecting wages and employment opportunities of U.S citizens. Even though the 22-year-old program ended, the aftermath created a migration pattern to and from the United States. Mexican citizens continue to travel to the United States because they needed to sustain their families. This caused them to go ahead and go back to the same fields even though they were getting abused. The abuse they sustained were from the same owners who wanted their cheap labor that way they can gain more profits rather than hiring native-born Americans who many cost them more of their profits.

Due to programs like the Bracero Program, and the establishment of the migration patterns, we know many undocumented individuals work in the agricultural sector in the United States. 73% of farmworkers are immigrants according to The National Agricultural Worker Survey. The demand for cheap labor from American companies is caused by Americans' lack of interest in working in the agricultural sector. Even applying the idea of 'supply and demand' could not help these companies fulfill Americans food demands without undocumented workers out on the fields. Raising wages and benefits to become more appealing to citizens has not worked and is now affecting these companies. Companies going under will become the reality for many business owners because of how eager the Trump administration is to deport undocumented workers. However, to be fair to the Trump administration, the policies allowing for mass deportations were prepared before he assumed office. One of them being is taking advantage of is the Illegal Immigration Reform and Immigrant Responsibility Act (IIRIRA).

For example, the Illegal Immigration Reform and Immigrant Responsibility Act (IIRIRA) is the bipartisan bill signed by President Bill Clinton that makes deporting undocumented workers much easier. This law created the foundation for the deportation machine we know today. Its increased penalties and the type of crimes any immigrant that violates "moral turpitude" meaning any behavior that violates the standard of the community. This applied to every undocumented worker and legal permanent resident, they can all face deportation for any non-violent crime. It also allowed for detaining and deporting individuals without due process. IIRIRA made it nearly impossible for undocumented individuals seeking legal status, to receive it because they needed to show "extreme hardships" cause to become a U.S Citizen through a process called "cancellation of removal." Even if a judge grants their case, there is still a cap on how many individuals can adjust their status per year. These provisions on the law have and will continue affecting companies who rely on cheap labor brought by undocumented individuals because of the xenophobia rhetoric being spewed by the current administration.

The deportation enforcement being promised by the United States government will massively affect the agricultural sector. It will cause the prices of fruits and vegetables to soar, and, as mentioned above, will lead to a labor shortage as Americans refuse to work in this sector of the economy. We must understand that undocumented workers within agricultural sectors, and outside of it, need protections and bargaining power if they are to continue to help sustain the U.S economy.

Therefore, we need to reform visas such as the guest worker program or the H-2A, which allow U.S farmers to hire workers temporarily when there are not enough workers in the United States. However, as noted above, there are problems with programs, such as the Bracero Program, which exploit the immigrant labor force. Abused by their employers, and working deplorable conditions, immigrants are taken advantage of by employers who know they will face few consequences because foreign workers lack an understanding of their rights as workers. Thus, workers are robbed of their wages, through underpayment or the use of hourly wage rates that push workers to work faster. Workers are afraid to get fired and deported back to their native country if they speak out. They are also not allowed to change their employer if they are unhappy with the conditions, they are accepted in. As a result, we see that the extent of the exploitation of foreign-born workers reaches unimaginable depths once you start scratching the surface of this visa program.

We need a better system than what we currently have. The United States has proven how much they love immigrants when it's convenient, but their xenophobia always reappears in their handling of the policies surrounding immigration. We can see it in the way local businesses treat their employees, and in large corporations exploiting cheap labor overseas. America hates it when immigrant workers start fighting for their rights and for the end of their exploitation, and as a result, we must protect these workers who are a vital part of our economic stability. We need to establish protection for workers who are repeatedly exploited by their companies. These individuals are doing important jobs for low pay, and they are subjected towards inhumane treatment by a country who treats them as if they are disposable.[30]

A study made by the Center for Migration Studies (CMS) found the following facts:

Agricultural workers in the United States not only support the US economy, but are also responsible for keeping people across the country and the globe fed. The agricultural sector contributed $1.055 trillion to the US GDP in 2020, with $134.7 billion coming just from farms. US agricultural exports were worth $139.6 billion in 2018.

The agricultural sector in the United States relies on foreign workers; 86

---

[30] SOSA Salma. Roosevelt House. Public Policy Institute at Hunter College, Without Undocumented Workers, the U.S Economy Would be a Disaster. March 24, 2020. Visited 10/23/2023. Available at: http://www.roosevelthouse.hunter.cuny.edu/?forum-post=witho ut-undocumented-workers-u-s-economy-disaster

percent of agricultural workers in the United States are foreign-born and 45 percent of all US agricultural workers are undocumented. Seasonal and agricultural labor demands are also growing in the United States. Requests for the H-2A Temporary Agricultural Worker Program, which brings immigrants from abroad for periods of up to eight months to meet agricultural workforce needs, have more than doubled from 2010 to 2019. The program increased from 79,000 H-2A workers in 2010 to 258,000 in 2019.

CMS estimates characteristics of populations who would be eligible for general and population-specific legalization programs and for special legal status programs. Due to the cyclical nature of agricultural work, it can be difficult to estimate the exact numbers and characteristics of workers with an annual survey.

According to CMS estimates, there are approximately 283,000 undocumented immigrants who work in the United States as agricultural workers. These individuals make up approximately 4 percent of the total undocumented workforce in United States. Immigrants coming from Mexico comprise the majority of undocumented agricultural workers at 88 percent. Following Mexico, undocumented agricultural workers come from Guatemala (7 percent), El Salvador (3 percent), Honduras (2 percent), and Nicaragua (1 percent). Approximately 63 percent of undocumented agricultural workers are male, and 37 percent are female.

According to CMS estimates, approximately 71 percent of this population has been living in the United States for more than 10 years. The top five states hosting the largest share of undocumented agricultural workers are:
California (49 percent)
Washington (9 percent)
Florida (7 percent)
Texas (5 percent)
Oregon (4 percent)
California, which hosts nearly half the undocumented agricultural worker population, is also the largest producer of cash farm receipts in the United

States, responsible for 13.7 percent of the US share in 2020.[31]

> *Nationwide, the hourly wages of immigrants are 12% lower than the hourly wages of American-born workers. In California, the wage gap is much larger (26%). But for immigrants in California with college degrees the wage gap is much smaller (8%) than for those with high school diplomas or less (27%). On average, immigrant workers' wages do not catch up to native-born workers' wages over time. But they tend to grow at a faster rate initially, increasing as much as 9% more quickly than comparable native-born workers' wages over the first 10-15 years after migration.[32] Immigrants and the Labor Market by Sarah Bohn and Eric Schiff*

How our immigration system can be exploited to suppress wages

Unauthorized immigrants are easily exploited by employers. Unauthorized immigrants, who make up nearly 5% of the U.S. labor force, contribute to the economy in vital industries and pay billions in taxes and contributions to the social safety net. But these eight million workers are not fully protected by U.S. labor laws because of their precarious immigration status: Unauthorized workers are often afraid to complain about unpaid wages and substandard working conditions because employers can retaliate against them by taking actions that can lead to their deportation. That also makes it difficult for unauthorized immigrants to join unions and help organize workers. This imbalanced relationship gives employers extraordinary power to exploit and underpay these workers, ultimately making it more difficult for similarly

---

[31] ROSENBLOOM, Raquel. Center for Migration Studies (CMS). A Profile of Undocumented Agricultural Workers in the United States. Visited 10/23/2023. Available at: https://cmsny.org/agricultural-workers-rosenbloom-083022/

[32] BOHN, Sara and SCHIFF, Eric. Public Policy Institute of California (PPIC). Immigrants and the Labor Market. March 2011. Visited 10/23/2023, Available at: https://www.ppic.org/publication/immigrants-and-the-labor-market/

situated U.S. workers to improve their wages and working conditions.

The exploitation described here is not theoretical. A landmark study and survey of 4,300 workers in three major cities found that 37.1% of unauthorized immigrant workers were victims of minimum wage violations, as compared with 15.6% of U.S.-born citizens. Further, an astounding 84.9% of unauthorized immigrants were not paid the overtime wages they worked for and were legally entitled to.

Migrant guestworkers are also vulnerable. One of the main authorized or "legal" pathways for migrants who want to work in the United States is via "nonimmigrant" visas that authorize temporary employment. The United States issues hundreds of thousands of nonimmigrant visas to workers from abroad every year in an alphabet soup of temporary work visa programs. Approximately 1.4 million guestworkers were employed in the United States in 2013 through work visa programs, accounting for roughly 1% of the labor force at the time. Although they are legally authorized to work, guestworkers are among the most exploited laborers in the U.S. workforce because the employment relationship created by the visa programs leaves workers powerless to defend and uphold their rights.

The abuses often start before guestworkers even arrive in the United States—many are required to pay exorbitant fees to labor recruiters to secure U.S. employment opportunities, even though such fees are usually illegal. Those fees leave them indebted to recruiters or third-party lenders, which can result in a form of debt bondage. After arriving in the United States, guestworkers may find out the job they were promised doesn't exist. And in a number of cases, guestworkers have become victims of human trafficking— with some being forced to work in the sex industry.

It's not just farmworkers and other lesser-skilled guestworkers suffering from the epidemic of fees, shady recruiters, and trafficking in temporary work visa programs: College-educated workers in computer occupations, as well as teachers and nurses, have been victimized and put in "financial bondage" by recruiters and staffing firms that steal wages and file lawsuits against workers if they try to quit.

Guestworkers who are in debt are anxious to earn enough to pay back what they owe and hopefully make a profit and are thus unlikely to rock the boat at work when things go wrong on the job. But even guestworkers who aren't caught in the debt trap are still subject to exploitation once they are working in the United States. Like unauthorized immigrants, guestworkers have good reason to fear retaliation and deportation if they speak up about wage theft, workplace abuses, or other working conditions like substandard health and safety procedures on the job—not because they don't have a valid immigration status, but because their visas are almost always tied to one employer who owns and controls their visa status. That visa status is what determines the worker's right to remain in the country; if they lose their job, they lose their visa and become deportable. This arrangement results in a form of indentured servitude. Further, employers can punish guestworkers for speaking out by not rehiring them the following year or by telling recruiters in countries of origin that they shouldn't be hired for other job opportunities in the United States (effectively blacklisting them).

The specter of retaliation makes it understandably difficult for guestworkers to complain to their employers and to government agencies about unpaid wages and substandard working conditions. Private lawsuits against employers who break the law are also an unrealistic avenue for enforcing guestworker rights, for two reasons: First, most guestworkers are not eligible for federally funded legal services under U.S. law, and second, guestworkers who have been fired are unlikely to have a valid immigration status permitting them to stay in the United States for long enough to pursue their claims in court.

Because of these conditions, temporary work visa programs have been dubbed "close to slavery," and government auditors have noted that increased protections are needed for migrant guestworkers.

Migrant guestworkers can be legally underpaid. To add insult to injury, there is abundant evidence that the laws and regulations governing major temporary work visa programs—such as H-2B and H-1B—permit employers to pay their guestworkers much less than the local average wage for the jobs they fill. And most work visa programs have no minimum or prevailing wage rules at all—maybe that's why some employers think they can get away with vastly underpaying their guestworkers, as one Silicon Valley technology company in Fremont, California, did by paying less than $2 an hour to skilled migrant workers from India on L-1 visas who were working up to 122 hours per week installing computers.

While employers are still required by law to pay guestworkers at least the state or federal minimum wage, that's often far less than the true market rate, or the local average wage, for the occupation they're employed in. The company employing the L-1 guestworkers in Fremont who were paid less than $2 an hour got in trouble because California law required that they be paid no less than $8 an hour (the state minimum wage at the time) plus time-and-a-half for overtime. But the average wage in Fremont for the job they were employed in—installing computers—was $20 per hour at the time according to U.S. Department of Labor data, and if they were also configuring the computers for the company's network, they deserved to be paid $44 per hour. In the end, the company was required to pay back wages of $40,000 plus a fine of $3,500 "because of the willful nature of the violations"—a slap on the wrist considering the egregiousness of the wage theft and hardly a disincentive against future violations.

In essence, these visa programs are intentionally designed to create a labor market monopsony for employers—awarding employers greater leverage over their workers—and growing research has shown that even modest amounts of employer monopsony power are utterly corrosive to workers' ability to bargain for better wages.

Visa program rules make it easy for employers to avoid hiring U.S. workers in favor of exploitable and underpaid guestworkers. While two of the major U.S. work visa programs require that employers first recruit U.S. workers and offer them jobs before hiring guestworkers, the vast majority of the programs have no such requirement. That means that employers hiring through large work visa programs like the J-1, L-1, and H-1B can bypass the local workforce altogether when hiring migrant workers, regardless of whether the local area is experiencing high unemployment.

Even when employers are required to recruit locally, many go to great lengths to avoid employing U.S. workers—preferring to hire guestworkers because they can be more easily exploited. As the New York Times, Washington Post, and Vox have reported, some of President Trump's companies have taken measures to avoid hiring local U.S. workers so they can hire guestworkers.

When rules requiring recruitment of U.S. workers aren't in place, sometimes the abuses are even more egregious. There are many documented cases in which hundreds of U.S. technology workers were replaced with workers on H-1B visas earning tens of thousands of dollars less per year—and the U.S. workers were required to train their H-1B replacements to do their old jobs as a condition of receiving severance pay.

Oversight is lacking. There is also very little oversight of temporary work visa programs. Most of the programs have no rules in place at all to protect guestworkers after they arrive in the United States. Where such rules are in place, enforcement is woefully inadequate—and companies that are frequent and extreme violators of these rules are often allowed to continue hiring through visa programs with impunity.

Considering how these programs operate and the situation they leave guestworkers in, perhaps it is no surprise that less-skilled legal guestworkers earn approximately the same low wages on average that unauthorized immigrant workers do for similar jobs, despite the fact that unauthorized workers have virtually no rights in practice. In other words, these guestworkers don't have any financial incentive to work legally through visa programs since there is no wage premium for it—and, in fact, authorized guestworkers can end up worse off economically than unauthorized workers because of the debts they incur through fees paid to recruiters.[33]

---

[33] COSTA Daniel. Economic Policy Institute. Employers increase their profits and put downward pressure on wages and labor standards by exploiting migrant workers. Visited 10/23/2023. Available at: https://www.epi.org/publication/labor-day-2019-immigration-policy/

Money Remittances Fees

We estimate that in 2023, the industry will net revenues of $37.18 billion in fees consumers pay to send money. April 14, 2023. Insider Intelligence

How are these guys making that kind of money? because of the immigrants' remittances back to their countries.

An article published by the World Economic Forum, stablished that in 2022, migrant workers sent home almost $800 billion.

Figure 1.1a Remittances, Foreign Direct Investment, Portfolio Flows, and Official Development Assistance Flows to Low- and Middle-Income Countries, 1990–2023f

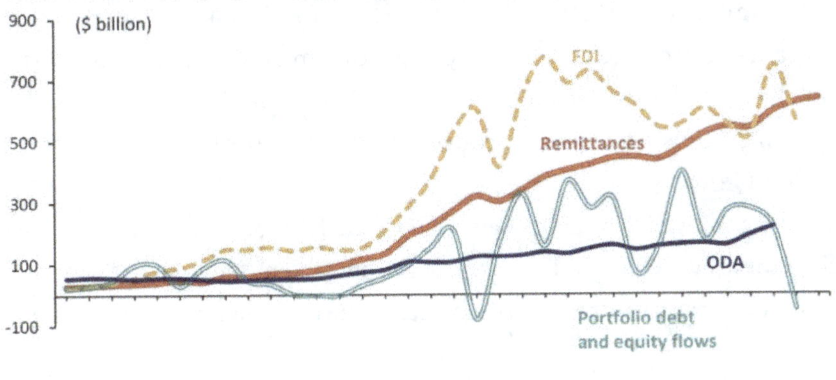

Remittances are a substantial source of external finance in low and middle-income countries. Image: WorldBank/Knomad

Money sent home by migrant workers is a lifeline to people in low and middle-income nations, and new data shows that the amount sent to these countries in 2022 is estimated to have risen by almost 5% to $626 billion.

Not all remittances are sent from rich to less well-off nations. The Russian invasion of Ukraine caused the amount of money sent home by Ukrainians living abroad to rise sharply, pushing total worldwide remittances to $794 billion, according to the World Bank.

If China is excluded from the calculation, remittances are the largest source of external finance in low and middle-income countries, exceeding the value of foreign direct investment and official development aid, the World Bank says.

The top five nations for remittances in 2022 are expected to be India (topping $100 billion for the first time), Mexico ($60 billion), China ($51 billion), the Philippines ($38 billion) and Egypt ($32 billion).

Mexico is seen overtaking China – which was in second position in 2021 – partly as a result of the strength of the US dollar, the World Bank said. Pakistan received $29 billion while Bangladesh and Nigeria each received $21 billion.

Remittances contribute 50% of the GDP of Tonga, 38% of GDP in Lebanon, 34% in Samoa, 32% in Tajikistan, 31% in Kyrgyzstan and more than a fifth of GDP in Gambia, Honduras, El Salvador, Haiti and Nepal.

"Migrants contribute massively to their origin countries by transferring financial and social remittances, encouraging trade linkages and making investments," says the World Economic Forum report Migration and Its Impact on Cities.

Almost 8 million Ukrainians have fled to the European Union since Russia attacked their homeland in February 2022, and the money they've sent home has boosted total remittances to countries in Europe and Central Asia by 10.3%.

The true value of remittances may be up to 50% higher than the official figures suggest because people often prefer to use informal methods to send money that are not recorded by the authorities, the IMF says.

The World Bank's analysis of the 2022 figures says that officially recorded remittance volumes have declined in countries that suffer from a shortage of foreign exchange and have multiple exchange rates, as people use alternative routes offering better exchange rates.

The cost of sending a $200 remittance to a low or middle-income country through officially approved routes averaged 6% of the total in the second quarter of 2022, it says. This was double the level set out in the United Nations' Sustainable Development Goals.[34]

Remittance facts

Remittances continue to matter more than ever. Here are some reasons why.

- A staggering one billion people worldwide – about one in eight – depend on remittances. Every year, 200 million migrant workers send money home, and 800 million people benefit from them.
- Even through a pandemic and political instability, remittance flows continued to grow. According to the latest World Bank data, remittances to low- and middle-income countries reached US$647 billion in 2022. That's a growth of 8 per cent compared to 2021 – higher than the World Bank expectations six months ago.
- Migrant workers send on average US$200 to US$300 home every one to two months. This represents only 15 per cent of what they earn – the rest stays in their host countries. But what they do send can make up as much as 60 per cent of a household's total income – representing a lifeline for millions of families.
- Over the last 20 years, remittance flows have grown in value five-fold, despite the myriad of adverse events that took place all over the world.
- The amount of money sent via mobile transfer increased 65 per cent during 2020 to US$12.7 billion and grew again to US$16 billion in 2021.

---

[34] BROOM Douglas. World Economic Forum. Migrant workers sent home almost $800 billion in 2022. Which countries are the biggest recipients?. February 2, 2023. Visited 10/23/2023. Available at: https://www.weforum.org/agenda/2023/02/remittances-money-world-bank/

- Over 50 per cent of remittances are sent to rural areas, where 75 per cent of the world's poor and food-insecure live. Globally, the accumulated flow to rural areas is expected to reach approximately US$3 trillion over the next five years.
- About 75 per cent of remittances are used to put food on the table and cover medical expenses, school fees or housing expenses. In times of crisis, migrant workers are likely to send more money home to cover crop losses or family emergencies. The remaining 25 per cent of remittances, representing over US$150 billion per year, can either be saved or invested in asset-building or activities that generate income and jobs.
- More than 70 countries rely on remittances for at least 4 per cent of their GDP. As these countries demonstrate, remittances are an engine of socio-economic growth and transformation – particularly for rural areas.
- Remittances can be costly to send – and technical innovations like blockchain and mobile money might be the solution to keeping costs down. Right now, currency conversions and fees take up about 6 per cent of the total amount sent – that's double the 3 per cent target set by the Sustainable Development Goals (SDG). In this regard, there's enormous potential for innovative digital financial services.
- Between 2022 and 2030 –the SDG target year– an estimated US$5.4 trillion will be sent by migrant workers back to their communities of origin. Of that amount, around US$1.5 trillion will be either saved or invested.
- Migrant workers make an invaluable contribution to SDGs through remittances and investments. In particular, they contribute to ending poverty and hunger; promoting good health, quality education, clean water and sanitation, decent work and economic growth; and reducing inequalities.
- Strategic partnerships and progress on remittances go hand in hand. Partnerships among public and private sector stakeholders have paved the way for lowering the cost of remittance transfers and provided financial services for migrants and their families.

Digital remittances have the power to help transform rural economies while also reducing costs for remitters and enabling beneficiaries in rural areas to track and access funds quickly without having to travel long distances.[35]

---

[35] IFAD. 13 reasons why remittances are important. June 16, 2023. Visited 10/23/2023. Available at: https://www.ifad.org/en/web/latest/-/13-reasons-why-remittances-are-i mportant

Autocrats parasites

More people than ever are migrating worldwide, with millions of people sending home record amounts of cash that fund small businesses in Uganda and feed families from Ecuador to Nepal.

But the remittances also provide critical support to fragile states and autocratic regimes which rely on money earned by their citizens abroad to keep their economies afloat.

In Venezuela, a third of households depend on money transferred home from the more than 7.3 million migrants who fled the country's economic collapse, according to the Inter-American Dialogue policy group in Washington. In Central Asia, where many former Soviet officials' rule, migrants send so much money that the funds cover their nations' trade deficits, economists say. In Nicaragua, remittances have become so vital to the tax revenue of President Daniel Ortega's regime that some economists say reducing the flow of the funds would be a form of political resistance.

"If you didn't have remittances, the national economy would collapse," said Enrique Sáenz, an exiled Nicaraguan economist. "And in macroeconomic terms, Ortega would be in deep trouble."

The growing flow of money creates a challenge for reformers seeking to exert economic pressure on autocratic leaders. But limiting remittances would hurt the vulnerable families of migrants who remain back home and reliant on money transfers.

"Remittances are one of the most difficult issues we can deal with," said Ryan Berg, a political scientist at the Center for Strategic and International Studies in Washington. "Nobody really wants to touch that issue because who would ever, from a policy standpoint, try to interfere with remittances as a point of pressuring dictatorships when we all know people are suffering."

Since 2010, remittances to the developing world have nearly doubled, rising to a record $647 billion last year, more than foreign direct investments to those countries and more than international development aid, according to the World Bank.

In Nepal, a young and fragile democracy where remittances account for close to a quarter of GDP, inflows from migrant workers have helped keep a lid on bubbling anger at the government over its handling of the pandemic and a recent recession, said Jeevan Baniya, an expert on migration at the Kathmandu-based research institute Social Science Baha.

"Had it not been for the inflow of remittances, we would have likely experienced some kind of social or political upheaval," Baniya said. "Remittances end up reinforcing the existing power structure."

In Egypt, money sent by migrants provides three times more revenue than the government takes in from the state-owned Suez Canal, while remittances to Mexico surpassed the dollars generated by international tourism and oil exports.

"Remittances have become a financial lifeline for developing countries," said Dilip Ratha, a World Bank economist and remittances expert.

The millions of money transfers a year, each one often just a few hundred dollars at a time, are being spurred by soaring migration to the U.S. and Europe since the Covid-19 pandemic. Migrants are arriving in affluent countries that have labor shortages, allowing them to find higher-paying jobs and send more money home.

Some economists say that if remittances become too big, they can hurt longer-term development and create governance problems.

Connel Fullenkamp, a Duke University economist, said remittances can start to become problematic once they go above 5% to 10% of a nation's gross domestic product. The money can reduce incentives to work for those who receive the funds, he said. They can also curb demands on the government to fix domestic problems that cause migration in the first place.

"If you get remittances, it causes you to care less about what is really going on in your own backyard, because you can always tap your relatives overseas for more transfers," said Fullenkamp, who has written studies on remittances for the International Monetary Fund. "Politicians are well aware."

Some of the world's most remittance-dependent nations are ruled by autocratic regimes where people have few economic opportunities—save for leaving.

"These countries have stronger currencies than they would otherwise have, and they have less inflation than what they would otherwise have," said Roman Mogilevskii, an economist at the Philippines-based Asian Development Bank.

In the Central Asian nation of Tajikistan, money from migrants mainly working in Russia make up close to half of the country's GDP, according to the World Bank.

Remittances there have helped authoritarian President Emomali Rahmon maintain his three-decades-old grip on power, according to scholars on the country. Navruz Nekbakhtshoev, a political scientist from Tajikistan who lives in Nebraska, said the remittances calm grievances and demands on officials by feeding families back home. The mass outflow of young people to fund the cash flow also removes people who might otherwise challenge the political status quo.

"It works to stabilize the regime," he said. "As long as this exit path exists for the people, the autocratic regime can basically stay in power."

With Russia's economy struggling because of the war in Ukraine and Western sanctions, migrants could have fewer job opportunities, affecting remittances, economists say.

That is prompting Tajikistan and other Central Asian governments to try to reduce their dependence on Russia by promoting migrant paths to other places such as Turkey and England, said Zachary Witlin, an expert on the region at the Eurasia Group.

In fragile, democratic countries, a large drop in remittances can contribute to unrest. In Sri Lanka, where more money arrives from the diaspora than what is earned from tea exports, remittances fell by nearly half from 2020 to 2022. That contributed to a balance-of-payment crisis that drained the country's foreign-exchange reserves and left it unable to pay for imports or service its external debt. Amid mass unrest, the president fled the country last year.

Elsewhere, a decline in remittances could just push more people to leave as rulers repress dissent.

Cuba first allowed remittances after the unraveling in the 1990s of its benefactor, the Soviet Union, brought about a sharp economic contraction. The Western Hemisphere's lone Communist country realized that allowing some people to leave could serve as an important source of hard currency, historians say.

"Remittances can in some ways grease the wheel of a system that doesn't work," said Ted Henken, author of books on Cuba and a professor at New York's Baruch College. "A Cuban in Miami or Madrid might be worth more to the Cuban government just in terms of GDP."

Then from 2019 to 2021, remittances to Cuba fell more than 70% as a result of the pandemic and tougher U.S. sanctions designed partly to block the Cuban military from profiting from the transfers. The Cuban military was taking a cut of the "well-intentioned, generous funds" that Cuban-Americans sent back to their families, then-Secretary of State Mike Pompeo said in 2020.

With tourism to Cuba also drying up, people took to the streets to demand an end to a regime in power since 1959.

Today, remittances remain far below prepandemic levels and Cuban immigrant families in the U.S. increasingly bankroll the departure of their relatives from the island, said Emilio Morales, president of the Havana Consulting Group, a Miami-based firm that tracks Cuba's economy.

"THE SITUATION IS SO CHAOTIC THAT PEOPLE PREFER TO INVEST IN GETTING THEIR FAMILY OUT OF CUBA," HE SAID.

In Venezuela, an economy that has contracted 75% over the past decade, remittances are crucial for the people who have stayed in the country under the autocratic and bankrupt government of President Nicolás Maduro, said Angel Alvarado, a Venezuelan economist at the University of Pennsylvania.

"You can ask, 'How are people not dying of hunger in Venezuela?'" Alvarado said. "The answer is that they have at least one child living abroad, sending money for food and medicine."

In Nicaragua, remittances more than doubled from 2018 to 2022 after President Ortega violently put down protests. This year, they are expected to account for about 33% of the country's GDP, one of the highest rates in Latin America, said Manuel Orozco, a Nicaraguan economist at the Inter-American Dialogue.

Marta Ortega, 45, a Nicaraguan who found work cooking in homes in Costa Rica, said she never considered her transfers could support a regime she opposes. She just wanted to help her mother.

"It wasn't a lot," said Ortega. "But it was really important."[36]

---

[36] DUBE, Ryan. The Wall Street Journal. August 6, 2023. Visited 10/23/2023. Available at: https://www.wsj.com/world/americas/record-amounts-of-money-sent-back-home-end-u paiding-autocratic-regimes-5bd9cdd9

Smugglers parasites

CNN, on the pen of Catherine E. Shoichet, published a study, stablishing that: migrants from Guatemala, Honduras and El Salvador spend $2.2 billion every year trying to reach the United States, and most of that money goes to smugglers, according to a new report.

The estimate of annual costs over the past five years, derived from surveys of thousands of households in those three Central American countries, paints a stark picture of the price of migration – and who's profiting.

"That is an extreme amount of money," MIT associate professor Sarah Williams said in a statement announcing the report's release. "That $2.2 billion is all paid for by the migrants themselves, so the risks, both in terms of debt and personal risk, is borne by the migrant."

The report – released this week by the Migration Policy Institute, the World Food Programme and the Civic Data Design Lab at the Massachusetts Institute of Technology – details motivations and costs of migration from the region.

Migrants from Guatemala, Honduras and El Salvador traveling outside legal channels with smugglers pay about $1.7 billion annually, the report says. Migrants who travel outside legal channels from those countries in caravans or alone shell out about $230 million every year. And those migrating via legal pathways spend about $240 million.

The large numbers are particularly significant when you think about where else that money could go, such as funding for development and public works projects, says Ariel Ruiz, lead co-author of the report and a policy analyst at the Migration Policy Institute.

"It's important not just to talk about the cost, but also to talk about the potential and opportunity that are being siphoned away," he says.

Paying smugglers is the costliest way to migrate.

In the past some researchers have arrived at even higher figures when estimating the size of the smuggling industry.

A 2018 UN report estimated the business of trying to get people into Mexico and the US illegally was worth about $4 billion annually.

To come up with the estimates included in this week's report, Ruiz says researchers surveyed thousands of households in the region to determine the average amount paid in their attempts to migrate to the United States, then extrapolated based on the numbers of people who migrated from El Salvador, Guatemala and Honduras.

On average, those surveyed reported that migrants who paid smugglers spent about $7,500, including the cost of food and travel in addition to smugglers' fees.

Migrants who traveled on their own or in caravans spent an average of $2,900 and those who used regular immigration channels, such as student visas or refugee resettlement, spent $4,500.

Some incur debt that can be difficult to pay off – especially if the migrants aren't successful in reaching the United States, the report notes.

Why do these migrants make the journey.

Among the other findings:

- The vast majority (92%) surveyed said economic reasons were behind decisions to migrate. Climate disasters, violence and food insecurity were other factors noted. The amount spent on migration is "a lot of money," Ruiz says, "but in perspective, the return on the investment is significant when so many of them are in such precarious conditions in their countries of origin."

- More people are considering migration. In 2021, survey respondents in 43% of households said they were considering international migration, compared to 8% in 2019. But only a fraction of households – 3% – reported they were making concrete plans to migrate.
- Nearly a third of households (29%) reported receiving money from migrants abroad. They described that money as a lifeline used to meet subsistence costs and immediate expenses.[37]

Darien INC

Julie Turkewitz along with Federico Rios from The New York Times, after months in the Darien Gap, published the result of their investigation, titled: "'A Ticket to Disney'? Politicians Charge Millions to Send Migrants to U.S." They reported the following:

Every step through the jungle, there is money to be made.

The boat ride to reach the rainforest: $40. A guide on the treacherous route once you start walking: $170. A porter to carry your backpack over the muddy mountains: $100. A plate of chicken and rice after arduous climbing: $10. Special, all-inclusive packages to make the perilous slog faster and more bearable, with tents, boots and other necessities: $500, or more.

Hundreds of thousands of migrants are now pouring through a sliver of jungle known as the Darién Gap, the only land route to the United States from South America, in a record tide that the Biden administration and the Colombian government have vowed to stop.

But the windfall here at the edge of the continent is simply too big to pass up, and the entrepreneurs behind the migrant gold rush are not underground smugglers hiding from the authorities.

They are politicians, prominent businessmen and elected leaders, now sending thousands of migrants toward the United States in plain sight each

---

[37] SHOICHET, Catherine E. CNN. Migrants from three countries paid $2.2 billion trying to reach the US. Most of it went to smugglers. November 24, 2021. Visited 10/23/2023. Available at: https://www.cnn.com/2021/11/24/us/central-american-migration-costs/index.html

day — and charging millions of dollars a month for the privilege.

"We have organized everything: the boatmen, the guides, the bag carriers," said Darwin García, an elected community board member and former town councilman in Acandí, a Colombian municipality at the entrance to the jungle.

The crush of migrants willing to risk everything to make it to the United States is "the best thing that could have happened" to a poor town like his, he said.

Now, Mr. García's younger brother, Luis Fernando Martínez, the head of a local tourism association, is a leading candidate for mayor of Acandí — defending the migration business as the only profitable industry in a place that "didn't have a defined economy before."

The Darién Gap has quickly morphed into one the Western Hemisphere's most pressing political and humanitarian crises. A trickle only a few years ago has become a flood: More than 360,000 people have already crossed the jungle in 2023, according to the Panamanian government, surpassing last year's almost unthinkable record of nearly 250,000.

In response, the United States, Colombia and Panama signed an agreement in April to "end the illicit movement of people" through the Darién Gap, a practice that "leads to death and exploitation of vulnerable people for significant profit."

Today, that profit is greater than ever, with local leaders collecting tens of millions of dollars this year alone from migrants in an enormous people-moving operation — one that international experts say is more sophisticated than anything they have seen.

"This is a beautiful economy," said Fredy Marín, a former town councilman in the neighboring municipality of Necoclí who manages a boat company that ferries migrants on their way to the United States. He says he transports thousands of people a month, charging them $40 a head.

Mr. Marín is now running for mayor of Necoclí, vowing to preserve the thriving migration industry.

"What was first a problem," he said of the many migrants who began showing up in the last few years, "has become an opportunity."

American diplomats have visited the towns next to the Darién Gap in recent months, strolling dusty streets and shaking hands with Mr. Marín, Mr. García and others running the migration business. White House officials say they believe that the Colombian government is following through on its commitment to crack down on illicit migration.

But on the ground, the opposite is happening. The New York Times has spent months here in the Darién Gap and surrounding towns, and the national government has, at best, a marginal presence.

When the national authorities can be seen at all, they are often waving migrants through, or in the case of the national police, fist-bumping the men selling expensive travel packages through the jungle.

The top police official in the region, Col. William Zubieta, said it wasn't his job to halt the flow. Instead, he argued, the nation's migration authorities should be exerting control.

"Unfortunately, they do not have it," he said.

Colombia's president, Gustavo Petro, acknowledged in an interview that the national government had little control over the region, but added that it was not his goal to stop migration through the Darién anyway — despite the agreement his government signed with the United States.

After all, he argued, the roots of this migration were "the product of poorly taken measures against Latin American peoples," particularly by the United States, pointing to Washington's sanctions against Venezuela.

He said he had no intention of sending "horses and whips" to the border to solve a problem that wasn't of his country's making.

In the absence of the Colombian government, local leaders have decided to handle migration themselves.

Today, the business is run by elected community board members like Mr. García, through a registered nonprofit started by the board's president and his family. It's called the New Light Darién Foundation, and it manages the entire route from Acandí to the border with Panama — setting prices for the journey, collecting fees and running sprawling campsites in the middle of the jungle.

The foundation has hired more than 2,000 local guides and backpack carriers, organized in teams with numbered T-shirts of varying colors — lime green, butter yellow, sky blue — like members of an amateur soccer league.

Migrants pay for tiers of what the foundation calls "services," including the basic $170 guide and security package to the border. Then a migration "adviser" wraps two bracelets around their wrists as proof of payment.

"Like a ticket to Disney," said Renny Montilla, 25, a construction worker from Venezuela.

Mr. García says that the foundation's work is legal, in part because it guides people to an international border, but not over one.

Some officials have questioned whether the foundation is running a smuggling operation under the guise of a nonprofit. A human rights officer responsible for monitoring the Necoclí government blamed the crisis on the negligence of national leaders and noted that officials weren't motivated to stop it because they were making money from it.

Even Mr. García's brother, the mayoral candidate, said he wished the national government would clarify the legal "thin line" that local residents working in the migration industry were walking.

"Five hundred thousand people are going to pass through" our town, Mr. Martínez said. "What do we do?"

Hanging over the entire business is a large and powerful drug-trafficking group called the Gaitanist Self-Defense Forces, sometimes known as the Gulf Clan. Its control over this part of northern Colombia is so complete that the country's ombudsman's office calls the group the region's "hegemonic" armed actor.

In a recent report, the ombudsman accused the group of exercising what it called "criminal governance" over the region, meaning that whatever happens here must have the group's blessing.

Mr. García, the community board member, acknowledged that the armed group "provides security" in the region, but insisted that the foundation was completely separate.

"I am not part of the Gulf Clan," he said.

In a statement, the armed group contended that it "in no way" profits from "the business that traffics in migrants' dreams."

Mr. Petro, the Colombian president, dismissed that notion, saying the Gulf

Clan was earning $30 million a year from the migration business.

At the edge of the forest, the transactions are plain to see.

Before they enter the jungle, migrants have to pay the group a separate tax of about $80 a person for permission to cross the Darién, according to multiple people who collect the fee in Necoclí.

Once migrants have paid, they even get a receipt, the tax collectors say: a tiny sticker, often an American flag, on their passports.

Taming a Jungle

Thick, hot and prone to intense rain, sliced by raging rivers and steep mountains, the Darién jungle acted as a vast natural barrier between North and South America for generations, thwarting the flow of people north.

Guerrillas and other armed groups have long used the dense forest for cover and drug smuggling, sometimes attacking those who dared to pass. The terrain and threat of violence once kept all but the most desperate away.

But a stew of crises and politics — like the turmoil in Venezuela, Haiti and now Ecuador, the economic devastation of the pandemic, and visa regulations that prevent many migrants from simply flying to Mexico or other countries — has brought a huge rise in the number of people trekking from South America to the United States in the last few years.

Now, the New Light Darién Foundation is helping to turn that natural barrier into something much more passable, with restaurants, camps, porters and guides.

This new economy, run in large part by elected leaders, has acted as an accelerant, emboldening more people to take — and pay for — the journey than ever.

In August alone, almost 82,000 people made the trek through the Darién, according to Panamanian officials, by far the largest single-month total on record.

So many people are coming through the jungle that Panama and Costa Rica say they cannot handle the surge. Panama's top migration official, Samira Gozaine, has even threatened to close its border with Colombia.

And the political tumult stacks up all the way to the United States. After dipping briefly this year, migrant apprehensions at the American border have risen again, with a record number of families crossing.

The Colombians transporting migrants through the jungle say they are providing a humanitarian service. The migrants will try to get to the United States regardless, they say, driven by violence, poverty and political upheaval at home.

So, by professionalizing the migration business, Colombian leaders say they can prevent their impoverished towns from being overwhelmed by hundreds of thousands of needy people, help the migrants traverse the treacherous jungle more safely — and feed their own economies in the process.

Migrant deaths in the Colombian portion of the Darién now appear to be relatively low, aid workers say, because even the Gaitanist armed group, or Gulf Clan, has realized that the Darién's notoriety is bad for business. Local officials say the group has set a policy to keep customers coming: Anyone who robs, rapes or kills a migrant will face punishment, possibly even death.

But the Daríen is still perilous, with diseases like malaria and dengue stalking migrants in "a grotesque test of survival," said Carlos Franco-Paredes, a doctor studying the journey.

Beyond that, the foundation's guides take migrants only part of the way, leaving them at the border with Panama, often with no food or money left — and days of hiking to go in a part of the jungle that is even more dangerous than what they already endured. The United Nations counted more than 140 migrants deaths in the Panama portion of the Darién last year alone, nearly triple the year before. At least 10 percent of them were children.

Mr. Petro, Colombia's first leftist president, came to office last year promising to help long forgotten parts of the country — like the communities now in charge of the jungle crossings.

In the interview, Mr. Petro said he had never heard of the New Light Darién Foundation. But just like the people running the migration business, he presented his hands-off approach to migration as a humanitarian one.

The answer to this crisis, he said, was not to go "chasing migrants" at the border or to force them into "concentration camps" that blocked them from trying to reach the United States.

"I would say yes, I'll help, but not like you think," Mr. Petro said of the agreement with the Biden administration, which was big on ambition but thin on details. He said any solution to the issue had to focus on "solving migrants' social problems, which do not come from Colombia."

He expects half a million people to cross the Darién this year, he said, and then a million next year.

On the other side of the Darién Gap, Panamanian officials are fuming, accusing "countries to the south" of shirking "their due responsibility" to stem the tide of people heading north.

"There is nothing humanitarian about this," Ms. Gozaine, the Panamanian migration official, said at a recent news conference. "The children who die in the jungle, the women who are raped, the men who are raped, the people who are killed."

Crisis, Then Bonanza

The boats leave each day from the eastern edge of Necoclí, the docks filled with people from around the world — not only from the Western Hemisphere, but from as far as India, China and Afghanistan.

"Travel safe!" Mr. Marín's employees boom from a microphone. "Travel happy!"

At his office, where a service award from the national police hangs on the wall, Mr. Marín said that he was proud to be a part of the industry that had become the region's most important employer.

Just outside, a new construction project soars, soon to be a gas station that will fuel his boats more quickly than ever.

Remote, tropical and bordering the Caribbean Sea, the Colombian towns on the migrant path to the jungle are beautiful but poor. More than half of their residents live below the poverty line. Many are victims of the country's decades-long war, forced to live among criminal groups for generations. Fishing, tourism and wildcat gold mining have long been among the main sources of income.

But in 2021, the towns started changing, quickly. Thousands of Haitians began showing up, fleeing the tumult that only worsened after the assassination of their president.

Suddenly, the region's already precarious sewage, water and electricity systems were overwhelmed. The beaches filled with migrant tents, pushing out an already struggling tourism industry.

The way local leaders tell it, pleas for help from the national government fell on deaf ears.

Mr. Marín, then a city councilman, was one of the first to do something big, turning crisis into opportunity by taking command of the boat company, Katamaranes S.A.S., with the goal of shuttling migrants to the Darién on their way to the United States.

Since then, Necoclí, once a sleepy beach town offering two-for-one cocktails, nature hikes and sea excursions for tourists, has been transformed.

At almost any hour, day or night, private buses wheeze into town, carrying migrants who have learned about the Darién route on Facebook, WhatsApp and TikTok, the de facto advertising services for the journey.

The streets of Necoclí are now filled with people speaking Mandarin, Persian and Nepali. Locals with wooden carts make a living selling flimsy tents, snake repellent and toddler-size rubber boots. Aid workers in canvas vests patrol the streets, offering a bit of help — water jugs, diapers, sunscreen.

A laminated instruction booklet tied to the register at a grocery store provides tips for crossing the jungle. A map marks in red the common locations of "violent assaults and rapes."

New hostels are everywhere. In a region so poor that horse carts still plod the streets, expensive motorcycles roar through town and $100,000 SUVs roll alongside the sea.

The poorest migrants arrive by foot, camping on the beach. Most come from Venezuela, which has been in the grips of an economic and humanitarian crisis for nearly a decade, with few signs that the country's authoritarian leader, Nicolás Maduro, will give up power any time soon.

Many of the Venezuelan migrants congregate outside a thatch-roof soup kitchen opened just a few months ago by an aid group. Here, children waiting for meals of beans and arepas bear the telltale signs of malnutrition: skinny limbs, hair turned rust yellow.

Francis Sifontes, 32, stood in the breakfast line. In Venezuela, she had made so little working for the government's signature food-distribution program that her husband had been forced to beg in the street.

Destitute, the family moved to Colombia, where they cut sugar cane, grueling work that paid $5 a day.

Ms. Sifontes had arrived in Necoclí three weeks before, with her husband, stepson and four young children. To earn money for the rest of the journey, they had found work in the region's new micro-economy, buying small goods in bulk from local merchants — plastic trash bags, cheap lighters — and selling them to other migrants for a profit of 20 or 30 cents a piece.

At night they slept in a single tent in the shadow of Mr. Marín's office.

But they were hopeful, Ms. Sifontes said, because they had recently struck a deal with Mr. Marín. If they cleaned the beach by his business, for an unspecified amount of time, she said, Mr. Marín had promised to give them three boat tickets to the Darién.

Darién Gap Inc.

Once across the choppy Gulf of Urabá, the passengers on Mr. Marín's boats arrive in the town of Acandí, at the mouth of the jungle. For decades, some residents here have led migrants into the jungle for a fee, arguing that people would die without help.

But with the arrival of the Haitians in 2021, and then an even bigger wave of Venezuelans in 2022, local leaders began to organize, bringing the migration business under the New Light Darién Foundation.

On a recent afternoon, Alexandra Vilcacundo, 44, traveling with 30 others fleeing the rising violence in Ecuador, stepped onto the wooden dock in Acandí. Ms. Vilcacundo, a seamstress, looked terrified, having left three children behind. "We know that we are risking our lives," she said of the journey ahead.

On the bus to Necoclí, she said they had been stopped five times by Colombian police officers who threatened to arrest them unless they paid bribes. (A dozen others said they had also been extorted by the police.)

Once loaded into motorized rickshaws, Ms. Vilcacundo and the other migrants were ferried through Acandí on dirt roads still flooded from the previous night's rain. They passed cow pastures and a corn field, before finally passing through a gate into a compound Mr. García called "the shelter."

There were no police, migration authorities or international groups present. To the contrary, an insignia — "AGC," the Spanish initials of the Gaitanist Self-Defense Forces, or Gulf Clan — had been painted on a wall on the way to the shelter, a reminder of who ultimately called the shots.

Roughly a thousand migrants had gathered inside the compound. Local men in skinny jeans, polo shirts and sunglasses roved the sun-beaten expanse, introducing themselves as the foundation's "advisers," in charge of collecting fees and describing the route from here.

For those who didn't have the money on hand, there was a Western Union agent inside the compound, charging 15 percent per transfer. (The company said it had agents in Acandí, but that anyone operating inside a migrant camp was doing so in an unauthorized way).

Mr. García of the community board showed off public works nearby, built by the board with funds from the migration business, he said: a foot bridge by the dock, a school in one of the area's poorest neighborhoods, meters of paved road, a drainage system so the town would not flood.

He said the town had spent decades trying to become a tourist destination. But for now, without decent schools, a hospital or even a road connecting it to the rest of the country, all it had was migration.

"What we have done" with migration is more than tourism brought "in 50 years," Mr. García said.

Sutures and Ice Cream

Few places embody the transformation of the Darién route like the first camp in the jungle.

Two years ago, the route from the shelter in Acandí to this camp, Las Tecas, was a crude dirt path. Today, it is a road navigable by truck. The camp itself was once a muddy expanse. Today it is a village, with a welcome pavilion, security checkpoint, 38 shops and restaurants, Wi-Fi and even a billiard hall.

Here, the New Light Darién Foundation has organized the vast teams of guides and backpack carriers in their numbered and color-coded T-shirts. A few have dressed up their uniforms further, adding words like "respect" and "friendship" to their sleeves.

The foundation coordinates their schedules to spread around the work

— guides get to make one trek every 15 days — and pays them $125 per trek. Porters are contracted individually by migrants who want help carrying their luggage or children, somewhere between $60 and $120 per load. Any employees who abandon or rob their charges are fired, said Mr. García.

"If I had not found this job, I have no idea how I would have sustained my family," said Aureliana Domicó, 32, a single mother who works as a backpack carrier, carting up to 70 pounds to the Panama border several times a week. Months ago, heavy rain wiped out her plantain crop, leaving her four children with nothing to eat. Now, she makes as much as $800 a month.

Elmer Arias, 29, a guide, had struggled to find work after losing an arm. He had punched a window in anger, and because there is no hospital in Acandí, it took him days to get care, eventually leading to an amputation. The migrants were not that different from him, he explained — reaching for better lives, "just like us."

At the Las Tecas welcome pavilion that evening, guides wanded the migrants with metal detectors, a new protocol.

"Razors?" one guide asked, confiscating anything sharp. "Knives? Machetes?"

The next morning, more than 2,000 migrants assembled in the heart of the camp. There were children in Barbie T-shirts, two anxious moms with toddlers on leashes, a man with a baby on his back and a doll tucked into his waistband, a woman with an American flag backpack.

Samuel, 13, wore a purple Lakers shirt. His mother, an elder care aide, had left Venezuela years before, moving from city to city in Colombia and Peru, trying to find decent work. She had spent the last of her savings on their tickets to the jungle.

To their right, the sun rose over the forest. To their left, guides and backpack carriers waited. The crowd buzzed with excitement.

Soon, a man from the foundation, Iván Díaz, climbed a hill above the camp, beginning the morning's orientation. This was not a race, he instructed on a megaphone. This was about surviving to make it to the United States.

Don't sleep by the rivers, he said; they often rise with the rain. Eat food with salt to prevent dehydration. Take breaks. Children should stay with their parents. Pregnant women should stick with the guides. Anyone caught with drugs would get sent back to Necoclí.

A bullhorn roared. "Applause!" Mr. Díaz shouted. The crowd cheered.

"Duro, duro, duro," he yelled — hard, hard, hard — "for Maduro, Maduro, Maduro!" he added, a sarcastic nod to the Venezuelan president.

The group laughed and booed.

"With God's blessing it will all go well," Mr. Díaz continued. "I know that in three weeks you will be sending me Western Union transfers from New York."

It was roughly a day and a half hike to the border with Panama, and along the way, the foundation had positioned small camps where migrants could buy water and food.

Prices rose as people climbed. A Gatorade costs $2.50 at the start, and $5 at the end. Ice cream sellers hiked with the crowd, coolers on their backs. At the bend of a river, the crowds were met by a man holding a platter of homemade empanadas for sale.

The migrants moved slowly, crisscrossing a river, climbing hills knotted by roots. With so many people, the traffic jam at times slowed to gridlock.

By midmorning, Natasha, 5, from Ecuador, slipped from the shoulders of a man who had been carrying her. Natasha came crashing down, slicing a spot above her eye on a rock.

She wailed in pain as blood gushed from her face. Her mother began to panic.

But up ahead, there was a nurse. In recent months, the New Light Darién Foundation has hired several nurses and a doctor to care for the migrants. In the absence of any other institutional presence, they had become a lifeline.

On the porch of a hut, the nurse, José Luis Fernández, cleaned the wound, injected an anesthetic and sutured the cut. "If it had hit a little higher," he said of the blow, "we could have been talking about a dead person."

Mr. Fernández used to work for a public hospital in nearby Turbo, he said, but left "for salary reasons."

The foundation pays him much more.

Most of the group slept that night in a crowded, muddy expanse known to the guides as the Fourth Camp, where a generator buzzed and several restaurants offered fried fish or chicken for $10 a plate, a small fortune for most of the migrants.

Many families, having spent all their money to get this far, ate nothing, wondering what they would do for the rest of the trek. At dusk, the camp smelled of human feces and gasoline. The mood began to shift.

In his tent, José García, 32, explained that he had already crossed the Darién last year, but had decided to turn around after it seemed the Biden administration would not let Venezuelans into the United States.

Now, he was trying again, this time with his wife, Dayarid Pernia, 24, and their two children, ages 1 and 3. But by this point, they were penniless.

He ruled the prices charged by the foundation to get this far.

"If this were humanitarian," Mr. García said of the route, his voice settling somewhere between a laugh and a cry, "they would lend a hand to those who have nothing."

The Handoff

For thousands of migrants, the normalization of this route has set up a cruel paradox.

On the Colombian side of the Darién, where the government is almost absent and the Gaitanist Self-Defense Forces, or Gulf Clan, dominate, crime in the jungle is lower, at least according to aid groups and researchers interviewing migrants at the end of the route.

That perception of safety is sending more and more people into the forest, believing that they will make it out alive.

But at the border with Panama, the foundation's guides leave them — crossing could lead to arrest — and the power of the armed group recedes. Then, on the Panamanian side, small criminal bands rove the forest, using rape as a tool to extract money and punish those who cannot pay.

The regional head of one aid group said that women and children are often the victims, with men forced to watch. Children as young as 6 have been shot and killed in this section of the jungle in the past year.

And anyone without money — including those who spent it paying guides in Colombia — is particularly vulnerable.

On their last morning in Colombia, the group of more than 2,000 migrants rose before dawn. Inside one of the restaurants, a few raised their hands in a pre-trek prayer.

"Thank you, Lord," said Nestor Fernández, 33, a Venezuelan who had been working construction in Chile. "Just as we submit to you, may everything that tries to rise against us submit — every robbery, every theft, every kidnapping, every killing."

In the darkness, the parade of people began their march to the border. Children held jugs of sugar water, which might be their only sustenance for days. A pregnant woman was helped out of the camp by two others, one on each side.

It took roughly two hours to climb two hills known as the Twins, and then they reached a muddy clearing with a hand-painted sign marking the border.

In the clearing, migrants still lucky enough to have money paid their porters. And then a man — one of the guides had introduced him as the "head of security," without elaboration — stepped forward to offer final instructions.

Move slowly, stick together and follow a route marked by blue and green pieces of plastic, he told the group. It would take three more days to reach the end of the jungle, he explained, where the United Nations and the government of Panama offered support.

"From the municipality of Acandí," he said before the migrants pushed on, "we would like to wish you a happy trip."[38]

---

[38] TURKEWITZ Julie and RIOS Federico. The New York Times. 'A Ticket to Disney'? Politicians Charge Millions to Send Migrants to U.S. September 14, 2023. Visited 10/23/2023. Available at: https://www.nytimes.com/2023/09/14/world/americas/migrant-business-dar ien-gap.html

IV

Breaking the glass ceiling

Migrant workers make an invaluable contribution to SDGs (Sustainable Development Goals) through remittances and investments. In particular, they contribute to ending poverty and hunger; promoting good health, quality education, clean water and sanitation, decent work and economic growth; and reducing inequalities.

Boost U.S. Economic Growth

Citizenship for Undocumented Immigrants Would Boost U.S. Economic Growth, is the title of the article published by Giovanni Peri and Reem Zaiour, where they gathered the following:

Putting undocumented immigrants on a pathway to citizenship would increase U.S. GDP by up to $1.7 trillion over the next decade, raise wages for all Americans, and create hundreds of thousands of new jobs, advancing the country's economic recovery.

Today, 10.2 million undocumented immigrants are living and working in communities across the United States. On average, they have lived in this country for 16 years and are parents, grandparents, and siblings to another 10.2 million family members. At the same time, it has been nearly 40 years since Congress has meaningfully reformed the U.S. immigration system, leaving a generation of individuals and their families vulnerable. Poll after poll has illustrated that the vast majority of Americans support putting undocumented immigrants on a pathway to citizenship. And as the nation emerges from the COVID-19 pandemic and looks toward the future, legalization is a key component of a just, equitable, and robust recovery.

As the Biden administration and Congress craft their recovery legislation and consider how best to move the nation's policies toward a more fair, humane, and workable immigration system, the Center for American Progress and the University of California, Davis's Global Migration Center modeled the economic impacts of several proposals that are currently before Congress. Using an aggregate macro-growth simulation, the model illustrates the benefits to the whole nation from putting undocumented immigrants on a pathway to citizenship. Such legislation would increase productivity and wages—not just for those eligible for legalization, but for all American workers—create hundreds of thousands of jobs and increase tax revenue.

To help inform policymakers and advocates, this report looks at four potential scenarios where Congress grants a pathway to citizenship to: all undocumented immigrants; undocumented immigrants working in essential occupations; Dreamers and those eligible for Temporary Protected Status (TPS); and a combination of Dreamers, those eligible for TPS, and essential workers.

The report finds that during the next decade:

Scenario 1: Providing a pathway to citizenship for all undocumented immigrants in the United States would boost U.S. gross domestic product (GDP) by a cumulative total of $1.7 trillion over 10 years and create 438,800 new jobs.

Five years after implementation, those eligible would earn annual wages that are $4,300 higher.

Ten years after implementation, those annual wages would be $14,000 higher, and all other American workers would see their annual wages increase by $700.

Scenario 2: Providing a pathway to citizenship for undocumented immigrants who are essential workers would boost the GDP by a cumulative total of $989 billion over 10 years and create 203,200 new jobs.

Five years after implementation, those eligible would experience annual wages that are $4,300 higher.

Ten years after implementation, those annual wages would be $11,800 higher, and all other American workers would see their annual wages increase by $300.

Scenario 3: Enacting the American Dream and Promise Act (H.R. 6) would increase U.S. GDP by a cumulative total of $799 billion over 10 years and create 285,400 new jobs.

Five years after implementation, those eligible would experience annual wages that are $4,300 higher.

Ten years after implementation, those annual wages would be $16,800 higher, and all other American workers would see their annual wages increase by $400.

Scenario 4: Providing a pathway to citizenship for H.R. 6-eligible and undocumented essential workers would boost the GDP by a cumulative total of $1.5 trillion over 10 years and create 400,800 new jobs.

Five years after implementation, those eligible would experience annual wages that are $4,300 higher.

Ten years after implementation, those annual wages would be $13,500 higher, and all other American workers would see their annual wages increase by $600.

Importantly, this analysis considers only these direct economic benefits. The model does not capture the potentially large additional benefits to eligible immigrants' children in education, health, and future productivity gains, as these effects would take place likely more than 10 years from implementation.

As the findings above show, creating a pathway to citizenship for undocumented immigrants not only is the right thing to do but also would be a substantial stimulus to the U.S. economy. Undocumented immigrants are critical to the nation's social infrastructure—a fact that has become even more widely understood amid the coronavirus pandemic. Across the country, they are building families and starting businesses, they are keeping hospitals open and functioning, and they are caring for Americans' loved ones. To that extent, legalization and a pathway to citizenship—which would raise wages for all workers, create hundreds of thousands of new jobs, and boost the GDP—is an investment in the country's infrastructure in and of itself. As the United States continues to address the coronavirus pandemic and works toward a just and equitable recovery, Congress must consider these proposals.[39]

---

[39] PERI Giovanni and ZAIOUR Reem. CAP Ideas Conference. Citizenship for Undocumented Immigrants Would Boost U.S. Economic Growth. Visited 10/23/2023. Available at: https://www.americanprogress.org/article/citizenship-undocumented-immigrants-boost-u-s-economic-growth/

About the Author

You can connect with me on:

🌐 https://juanrodulfo.com

🐦 https://twitter.com/rodulfox

📘 https://facebook.com/rodulfox

🔗 https://www.linkedin.com/in/rodulfox

🔗 https://www.instagram.com/rodulfox

Subscribe to my newsletter:

✉️ https://juanrodulfo.com

Also by Juan Rodulfo

Asylum Seekers

https://amzn.to/3yz0P9P

"Humans is the only specie on Earth, that Hunts, Tortures and Kills its own for Pleasure." What's wrong with humans? Is there anybody out there in Governments or Power Circles with some sense of respect for the Planet Earth and its inhabitants? By the time of publishing this book (November 2018) my Wife and I have known and helped more than hundred Venezuelan families in their Asylum Applications, including one family from Ecuador and other one from Colombia.

Why Maslow?

https://amzn.to/3yz0P9P

If the Governments in Association with Industry Leaders/Owners manage the wealth and Natural Resources around the world, then who is responsible of keeping the 80% of the Population dying of starvation and diseases on the two basic stages of the Maslow Pyramid of Needs?

Manual for Gorillas

https://amzn.to/3yz0P9P

A study by the Bertelsmann Stiftung has come to the conclusion that a billion more people live under dictatorship now than was the case 15 years ago. While the researchers concluded that the number of people living in democracies rose from 4 billion to 4.2 billion between 2003 and 2017, they also found that 3.3 billion people lived under dictatorship last year compared to 2.3 billion in 2003. The report further warned that growing restrictions on citizens' rights and legal standards was an acute problem in democracies.

Politics explained for Millennials

https://amzn.to/3yz0P9P

Presented in simple language, social media like format, the author offers the IMDb of politics, with digestible concepts, pictures, likes and dislikes to guide you to see politics the way your human and citizen condition must see it, with responsibility, awareness and conviction that your vote is your voice but only when given to the cause that really shares your interests, as planet earth inhabitant or else.

9 7 9 8 8 6 8 9 5 0 8 8 9